CLINICAL RESEARCHES

CONCERNING

THE HOMŒOPATHIC TREATMENT

OF

ASIATIC CHOLERA.

PRECEDED BY

A REVIEW ON THE ABUSE OF THE NUMERICAL METHOD IN MEDICINE.

BY

J. P. TESSIER, M.D.,

PHYSICIAN TO THE HOSPITAL SAINTE-MARGUERITE IN PARIS.

TRANSLATED

BY

CHARLES J. HEMPEL, M.D.,

FELLOW AND CORRESPONDING MEMBER OF THE HOMŒOPATHIC COLLEGE OF PENNSYLVANIA; HONORARY MEMBER OF THE HAHNEMANN SOCIETY OF LONDON, &C. &C.

NEW-YORK:

WILLIAM RADDE, 322 BROADWAY.

PHILADELPHIA: RADEMACHER & SHEEK.—BOSTON: OTIS CLAPP.—MANCHESTER, ENG.: TURNER, 41 PICADILLY.

1855.

HENRY LUDWIG, Printer, 45 Vesey-st.

ON THE ABUSE

OF THE

NUMERICAL METHOD IN MEDICINE.

I have stated in my " elementary principles" of homœopathy, that Hahnemann's method is systematically rejected by certain physicians for no other reason than because it is a theory. In the eyes of these learned men, every doctrine, every theory, every system is an obstacle to the scientific progress and development of medicine : hence according to their logic, Hahnemann's theory must necessarily be false and dangerous. Indeed, if every theory is necessarily false, there is no reason why Hahnemann's doctrine should be true.

The systematic opposition of these physicians to a philosophical reform of therapeutics, which seems to me fraught with great results, naturally leads me to examine this great question : Whence comes the truth in medicine ? Does it, as has been supposed, emanate from the men of genius who have successively produced their medical theories and systems ? or does it flow from the adoption of a certain logical method, as was proclaimed by Bacon, believed by Pinel, stated by Chomel, and repeated by Louis ?

The theory of knowledge is one of those questions which no one treats who is not either an accomplished metaphysician or a presumptuous ignoramus. I do not consider myself capable of judging between Aristoteles and Plato, Descartes and Bacon. In this respect I abide by the conclusions of the schools and of good sense ; this is sufficient for my purpose. Not being competent, I do not wish to meddle with the question of the origin of knowledge in its generality.

I shall content myself with examining whether the medical reformers who proscribe Hahnemann's ideas, because they did not come into the world as, according to their own infallible wisdom, they ought to have come, have or have not common sense on their side in what they themselves teach; in one word whether the method by means of which our observers and statistical philosophers pretend to reconstruct the medical edifice upon a new basis, is a serious truth or a utopia.

I shall say a few words of Pinel's endeavor to base medical science upon analysis; of Chomel's attempt to present a doctrine exempt from all theory; and lastly, I shall arrive at the medical reform of Louis, and shall dwell upon it at some length.

Pinel lived at a time when analysis was spoken of as we talk now-a days of progress, at a period when, in order to pass for a man of intellect, one had to be a friend of analysis as one has to be, in our time, a friend of progress. Pinel fell into the trap which the philosophical sophistry of his period laid to the simplicity of his genius. He imagined in good faith, but with a feeling of honest vanity, that, previous to his teachings, physicians had neglected analysis, because they made no more mention of it than they did of synthesis. He therefore betook himself to the task of basing medicine upon analysis, of declaiming without rhyme or reason against all theories, systems, flights of the imagination, premature conclusions, &c. But when he undertook to compose a book, the analysis remained outside on the cover, and the book was a synthesis or a nosological classification very much resembling that of Cullen. Moreover, Pinel believed in what he called the *eternal principles of the healing force of nature* which is as synthetical and hypothetical an idea as ever was. As a philosopher, Pinel is therefore without any merit, since he was unable, in the matter of method, to distinguish his right from his left hand. This does not take away his claim as a medical authority; but we cannot admit that it was his mission to direct the intelligence of the medical profession in a new channel of philosophy. To conduct others we must in the first place be able to walk without leading-strings. The reform of medicine by analysis is therefore an illusion which the spirit of the age rendered excusable.

Chomel who was an eminent practitioner and a distinguished pathologist, was frightened in his younger years by the impetuosity of Broussais, and this impression has clung to him all his life time. Seeing the pernicious influence which the theory of irritation had on the general science and practice of medicine, he conceived an aversion against all theories. He suspects every thing, which is not a simple isolated fact, or some direct inference from particular facts which it is easy to establish.

The dread of an evil frequently leads us to a worse one. Chomel arranged his personal impressions into an absolute system; this was an error. More than this; since it is just as impossible to do without theories as it is to live without air, and since Chomel is subject to the common laws of humanity, it follows that he has theories, that he propounds theories without knowing it, and that, in this respect, he lives in a complete illusion. I will proceed to the proof of this.

Chomel closes his "*Elements of general pathology*" with these words: "*our object* has been, we do not hesitate to to repeat it, to find the limits of our subject, to endeavor to reach them without going beyond them, and to present on an essentially abstract subject, *a doctrine exempt from theories,* and exclusively founded upon facts, and upon their immediate and rigorous consequences."

Here we have an author who is well convinced that he is no theorizer, that he has presented a doctrine free from theories, and who would blush to have followed a theory. This author does not even inquire whether there can be doctrines without theories, or, which is the same thing, whether it is possible to think without ideas. Well, let us examine his preface: "I have spoken of disease in general as I should speak of a particular case of disease, if I intended to give as complete a history of this case as it is possible to give . . . . . ." Hence Chomel's pathology is the description of some fictitious malady, a malady that comprises every thing which belongs to pathology and therapeutics, an imaginary being, in one word, a fiction; and this is no theory! Chomel is mistaken: it is not only a theory, but it is the oldest theory that has ever been known in medicine; it is the theory of the absolute unity of disease, of the unity of the pathological *type*. This theory is the opposite of that which teaches that every disease is an entity, and which therefore admits a plurality of types, and a radical distinction of these types in pathology. The theory of the absolute identity of all diseases, belongs both to the followers of Hippocrates and those of Broussais: the only difference existing between these two classes of philosophers is this, that, according to the hippocratists, disease is something general, a reaction of the vital principle, whereas the Broussaisists consider it as something Hippocrates teaches: fever is every thing; Broussais: irritation is every thing in pathology.

It is the application of the theory of the typical unity of all diseases to general pathology that Chomel calls a doctrine without theory. The pretension of furnishing a doctrine without a theory, is therefore an illusion just as much as the pretension of basing the medical edifice upon analysis; and, although excusable on account of the early impressions of the author, it is nevertheless an illusion, and not by any means a new guide to the activity of professional minds.

So far then we do not see that there exists a new method of discovering truth in medicine. And, if this new method does not exist, is it right to avail one's-self of some supposed truth as the exclusive condition of the perfection of art, for the purpose of proscribing the therapeutic reform of Hahnemann and those who wish to ascertain the truth or falsehood of this theory, precisely because it is a theory? It seems to me that, if it were possible to mistake an illusion for a new method, a new truth might easily be mistaken for an illusion.

I have now arrived at what I term the abuse of statistics in medicine, the so-called school of observation, the numerical method. I will at once explain why I look upon this method as an abuse of statistics.

From time immemorial observations and numbers have existed in medicine. From time immemorial there have been good and bad observers in medicine, and numbers have been resorted to for good and bad purposes; and the defect of a method being charged upon the inadequacy of those who apply it, and not upon the method itself, it has been supposed that the first scientific duty of a physician at all times was to observe, to observe unceasingly, and to meditate upon his observations rather than to count them. Indeed numbers will always be something secondary in medicine, but it would be wrong to reject them on this account, for they may be exceedingly useful in some cases. I have not the remotest thought of condemning numbers, no more than the exaggerated importance which is attached to them; this sort of extravagance is inherent in the very character of the numerical method, and is scarcely deserving of being noticed. The abuse to which I am desirous of calling the attention of physicians, is not exactly the tiresome and extravagant display of useless figures; but the fact, that the natural order of things has been inverted, and that the numerical method has been substituted in the place of the medical art.

This substitution constitutes the greatest possible abuse of statistics. This abuse is a characteristic feature of the School of observation, of the numerical School, of the statistical physicians, in one word, of those *observers* who oppose with all their might every endeavor to verify by observation Hahnemann's theory, because it is a theory. If we succeed in showing that this new basis upon which they attempt to construct the medical edifice, is a utopia, we shall be fully justified in pursuing other methods than those of our modern so-called *observers*; we shall be fully justified in not having adopted the sterile errors which these innovators offer as the source of all truth; in one word, in not having believed that it is possible in medicine to do without ideas, without theories, or doctrines, any more than without practical observation.

ASIATIC CHOLERA.

SEVENTEEN years ago I studied at the Hotel-Dieu, under Magendie, the Cholera, which then raged so fiercely in Paris. At that time I observed about seven hundred cases.* Another cholera-epidemic enabled us to make new observations. The interval between the two epidemics gave us time to reflect on the character of the disease. It is the result of these investigations that we now publish for the purpose of proving two things, first: that Asiatic Cholera is as well known to physicians as any other malady; secondly: that the treatment of this disease can be founded upon a truly scientific basis. These two propositions are opposed to the general opinion existing among laymen as well as among a large number of physicians. This seems to furnish an additional reason why these erroneous opinions, which are prejudicial to our art, should be removed.

It is not, by any means, my intention, to give a complete history of the cholera epidemic, from its origin. I shall confine myself to the principal points in the physiological, pathological and therapeutic analysis of the epidemic. This plan will enable me to treat a few of the serious questions that have been raised, and which, it seems to me, have not yet been satisfactorily solved. We shall perhaps likewise be enabled to draw the line of demarcation between what can be and what cannot be cured at the present day. In this way we shall point

* See Magendie, Lectures on Cholera at the Collège de France Paris, 1832, one vol. in 8.

out what has been done and what has yet to be done. It seems unnecessary to justify the plan of this work by any other reasons.

§I. PHYSIOLOGICAL ANALYSIS.

The question is not to give or to find a physiological definition of the Cholera that shall account for all its phenomena. Such an investigation, after straining our imagination to the utmost, would lead us where it has led all those that have given themselves up to it for the last twenty-four centuries, to a more or less ingenious methaphor. To my mind there is nothing less scientific than a metaphor, except the mind that contents itself with it. Let us send the physiological physicians, the organists, humoralists, chemiatrists, mechanical practitioners, &c., in search of the quintessence of Cholera; we will limit ourselves to the study of the phenomena that it presents to us.

Cholera assumes three different orders of symptoms, according as it attacks the animal, vital or natural functions.* The first manifest the invasion of the

* Here is a description of this traditional division of the functions, taken from the Latin of Bœrhaave:

"The functions are habitually distinguished into vital, natural and animal.

"*Vital* functions are such as are indispensable to the preservation of life; among these we number the muscular action of the heart, the secretory action of the brain, the pulmonary action, and the flow of the blood and of the vital spirits through those organs and their arteries, veins and nerves.

"*Natural* functions are those whose business it is to assimilate the food to the organs; these are the action of the viscera, vessels and humors, namely: the action of receiving, retaining, moving, changing, mixing, secreting, applying, excreting, consuming.

"*Animal* functions are so related to man that the mind either derives corresponding ideas from their action, or the will is influenced, or, stimulated into manifestation by this action; such functions are: tact, taste, smell, sight, hearing, perception, imagination, memory, judgment, reasoning, affections and voluntary motions." (H. Bœrhaave, Institutiones medicæ, Paris, 1747, p. 361—362).

disease by a sense of malaise, anxiety, aphonia, cramps, spasms, delirium, coma; the second by the thinness, frequency, smallness, irregularity, collapse of the pulse, the weakness of the beats of the heart, and the embarrassed respiration; the third by diarrhœa and vomiting, derangement of the secretions, some of which are entirely suppressed, by a sudden emaciation, by a suspension of the phenomena of nutrition, by coldness, blueness of the skin, hippocratic or choleric face, and this external appearance of the body which has been characterised by the equally correct and energetic appellation of *cadaverous.* To this group of symptoms we have to add congestions and inflammations that develop themselves before or after the febrile reaction, in order to have a complete aggregate of the phenomena that succeed each other with more or less regularity and connection in an attack of cholera, and the progressive aggravation of which brings the patients so frequently and so rapidly into the grave.

Whatever part of the body may be assaulted, the epidemic does not seem to confine itself to an alteration of the phenomena of sensibility and contractility. Its action is deeper; it taints the very sources of life, the essential, formative powers of the organism.

When the fundamental conditions of life are attacked, it is not only particular functions that are disturbed, but their whole relation to each other, their whole mechanism becomes deranged.

Animal functions.—It seldom happens that sensibility or contractility are the first functions that are attacked in cholera; it happens, however, in some cases. Thus, for instance, the disease has set in with cramps, pains, in various parts of the body, in the head, legs or in the extremities. More frequently, before experiencing any other pain, the patients experience a marked weariness and weakness in the muscles, a vague and general malaise. All this, however, occurs irregularly, and alterations in the animal functions do not always usher in the epidemic.

The seat of the cramps or pains varies; in some cases the extremities alone are attacked, in others the lumbar muscles or the large muscles over the thorax; the face and nape of the neck, and other parts are likewise invaded. When unremitting, the pains may become agonizing. Then they extort cries from the patients, and may even cause convulsive spasms. Almost all the patients retain their consciousness; the general sensibility is likewise preserved; the senses are but little or not at all impaired. In very serious cases they are rather duller; the hearing is rather hard, and the patient complains of buzzing; in almost every case there is loss of voice. At a later stage of the disease, delirium and coma set in.

Admitting that all these phenomena proceed from an alteration of the nerves of the animal sphere, what would be the seat of this alteration? The brain, the spinal marrow or the nerves? or would it in one case be one of these parts, and in another case another? And the muscles, are they affected directly or only indirectly in consequence of a counter-shock emanating from the alteration of the nerves that are ramified through their tissue?

The phenomena which we observe, are not sufficiently constant to be traced to the same portion of the nervous system. As regards the question whether the muscular irritability is affected primarily or secondarily, we are unable to affirm anything positive in this respect. Either of these two circumstances may occur. If we attempt to establish an order of succession in these modifications of the animal functions, two contrary opinions will likewise become apparent. Either the phenomena which seemed isolated at first, react, each in its way, upon the brain, and there become concentrated, or else the phenomena emanate from the cerebral mass as their focus, and localize themselves successively in the various elements of the animal functions. The specific mode of action as well as the unity of the nervous system, the double evolution of its phenomena from the centre to the periphery and from the periphery to the centre, do not permit any affirmation in this respect, for the positive demonstration of either of these mechanisms is impossible.

Vital functions. In the history of the vital functions we have to examine the blood-vessels, the circulation, the blood and respiration. The tone of the vessels is sensibly affected by the cholera. It is well known that their tone depends upon the voluntary expansion and contraction of their tissue. These properties are entirely different from their elasticity, which is not spontaneous. The coats of the veins are flabby, although these vessels are not empty. If a vein is opened, and the blood pressed out, the coats of the vein do not contract, they remain what they were. I do not know whether a similar phenomenon takes place in the arteries; inductive reasoning would seem to lead us to think so. The beats of the heart are weaker; its contractions seem without energy; they are not unusually excited by the obstacle which the capillary circulation seems to oppose; on the contrary, the action of the heart is just as depressed as that of the veins and arteries. It would seem as though the blood could not pass beyond the capillaries, for it accumulates in these vessels, especially in their terminal ramifications, and there produces these passive congestions, and this blueish color which are one of the characteristic signs of cholera. Generally however, when the blood does not flow to a part in sufficient quantity, without there existing any obstacle to the venous circulation, this part assumes a livid pallor.

The veins seem to swell, and the venous blood bears no proportion to the corresponding arterial blood.* In cholera a state of inertia prevails at the centre as well as at the periphery of the sanguineous system. The circulation is still going on even when the pulse has become imperceptible. This is evident from the fact that camphor or ether which has been deposited in a mucous bursa, is absorbed; but the circulatory movement is exceedingly depressed.

The blood is visibly altered in epidemic cholera. This alteration affects the proportion of the fluid to the solid constituents of the blood. Becquerel has furnished an interesting description of these alterations. Beside the chemical alterations, the blood presents altered physical and physiological properties. The first alteration, which was pointed out by Magendie in 1832, is the extreme viscidity of the blood during the disease as well as after death. This viscous blood does not turn red when exposed to the air; but if previously mixed with a certain quantity of water, it will then turn red when exposed to the air. This viscidity seems therefore to be owing to the absence of water, and to certain changes in the proportion of the solid constituents of the blood.

As regards the physiological alteration of the blood, consisting in the fact that it is no longer coagulable, it remains even after the addition of water, or after the blood has turned red. This is a most important phenomenon. It shows that the blood has lost its only vital property, its plasticity. This loss of plasticity corresponds to the loss of tonicity in the organized tissues; it is the cessation of the spontaneous molecular movement by means of which life becomes manifest according to

* Before making any artificial injections in animals, it is even useful to tie the arteries of the part that is to be injected, a few moments previous to the operation. By this means the part through which the tied artery courses, becomes bloodless.

its inherent quality. In severe cases of cholera this alteration develops itself progressively; it indicates a disorder that is carried to its extreme limits, since it is, so to say, the commencement of death.

Does this vital alteration of the blood take place directly, or is it the effect of the excessive alvine evacuations? If this latter supposition were true, the alteration of the blood could only take place after considerable discharges from the bowels had taken place. But it is seen even at the commencement of the disease, before the bowels had been much affected. I am therefore inclined to think that the alteration of the blood takes place directly, and that, on the other hand, the evacuations exercise a marked influence on the constitution of this fluid.

In its mechanical phenomena the respiration does not seem disturbed; but may we not suppose that the blood in the lungs remains unaltered? It would seem so, to some extent at least, since the arterial blood, during the course of the malady, is as black as the venous blood.

These extraordinarily rapid and deep alterations of the vital functions constitute one of the particular features of cholera; they do not exist to the same extent in any other disease.

Natural functions.—These functions are the first that become altered during an attack of cholera. This alteration exists in every stage and form of the disease. From the mouth to the anus, all the phenomena are modified; it is not only the secretions that are altered; the tissues are likewise changed by characteristic symptoms of inflammation. The most striking changes are excessive intestinal and gastric secretions, suppression of the bilious secretion after a few evacuations, and suppression of all the other secretions.

The altered appearance of the secreted substance indicates the derangement in the natural functions.

The unitary relation of the secretions shows itself by the suppression of some, and the excess of the gastro-intestinal discharges.

If sweat appears, it is only a partial sweat, in the face, on the extremities; the unity of the secretions is least perceived on the skin.

The external changes of the body are exceedingly remarkable. The totality of these changes produces the well known cadaverous aspect of cholera-patients. They show a deep alteration in the nutrition of the solids. The skin is either the seat of partial congestions in the face and at the extremities, or else extending all over the body; these congestions have a livid appearance. Simultaneously with the appearance of the congestions, the mucous membrane collapses, and the skin loses its tonicity. This coincidence of the congestions with the loss of tonicity and the diminution of animal heat in the affected parts, is a sign of a most violent attack on the vital forces; it is the sign of a death-struggle from the commencement of the disease.

In order to complete this physiological analysis of the morbid phenomena of the cholera and group them into a unit, it remains for us to determine their order of succession or mutual relations. This can only be done imperfectly, but it may be useful to make the attempt.

In cholera life is attacked to its very foundation, but not to the same extent in every case. The vital principle cannot be attacked in its very sources, in its formative power, without vital products manifesting a corresponding alteration. Indeed, in all the affected parts, we not only notice a functional derangement, but a perceptible alteration of nutrition and of the properties of these parts themselves. I have already pointed out the diminished tonicity of the tissues, and the diminished plasticity of the blood. These, however, are not the only alterations in the phenomena of reproduction, since simple irritations may be succeeded by real inflammations, the signs of which become more marked in proportion as the disease develops itself beyond its cold stage. The phenomena of cholera are different from the so-called nervous phenomena, which simply affect the surface of the vital functions. In cholera the depths of life itself seem to be tainted. The phenomena of irritability depending upon those of reproduction, it clearly follows that these must be succeeded by an altered sensibility and contractility in each of the various apparatuses attacked by the cholera. Here follows the order of succession in the phenomena of cholera as manifested in each of these parts.

The organs of the natural functions are always attacked, but they may be attacked alone. The derangement of the natural functions is generally succeeded by a derangement of the vital functions; in such a case the organs of the animal functions are scarcely ever left intact; sometimes the derangement of the animal functions even precedes that of the vital functions. These alterations vary through a whole series of degrees; they are either more marked in the natural, animal, or simultaneously in two of these three orders of functions. One may likewise cease whilst the other is just commencing, and the disease may thus attack one apparatus after the other, abandoning at least in a measure the former before it attacks the second, and the second before it passes to the third.

In some cases these three classes of apparatuses are struck simultaneously by the disease from its very commencement, and with an extreme violence. Not only may the organs of the natural, vital and animal functions be deranged, but the central nervous system which maintains the normal relation of these organs to each other, may likewise be attacked. If this happens, we observe in the production, succession and relation of the morbid phenomena those strange irregularities which are designated under the name of ataxic cholera.

Last question. How does death take place in cholera? We have seen that the phenomena of formation are intensely altered in an attack of cholera; we may therefore, conclude, that death takes place in consequence of the immediate lesion of the vital principle. As to the mode of dying, it varies according as the patient dies at one or the other period of the disease. In the cold stage the vital spark becomes extinct gradually and progressively; nevertheless death finally takes place when the irritability of the heart has become extinct, and its beats cease in consequence. The organs, in this case, present all the symptoms of death by syncope, as Bichat has described them, without, however, the characteristic cholera-changes being any the less on that account. After the reaction, death almost always takes place by the brain; but, since at the last moments, the alteration of the vital functions is combined with that of the central nervous system, and the coldness and blueness reappear with the cessation of the arterial pulsations, it follows that death takes place both by the derangement of the cerebral functions and by the discontinuance of the heart's action. Indeed the signs of death by the brain, and those of death by the heart, in other words the signs of asphyxia and those of syncope are found combined.*

I shall not carry the physiological analysis of cholera any farther. It may be said that this analysis does not shed any light on the inmost nature of cholera. This is true, but we ought not to ask of physiology what it cannot give us. Beyond analysis we have fancies, arbitrary hypotheses, illusions and deceptions. They

* See Bichat's *Investigations of life and death.* (Recherches sur la vie et la mort.)

all lead to extravagant conclusions, from which the cholera would not be an exception.

§ II. PATHOLOGICAL ANALYSIS.

The term *cholera* is thus defined by Boerhaave: *A violent evacuation from the stomach and bowels upwards and downwards.** If applied to the disease, whether epidemic or sporadic, of which we treat, the term *morbus* was originally added to it: cholera-disease, real cholera. The disease is, therefore, named, in accordance with its principal symptom. It is not my intention to describe it here in all its completeness, not having any thing to add which is not perfectly known to every body; I shall limit my pathological analysis to the forms which the cholera presented in 1832 and 1849. These forms were the same in both epidemics; the only difference consisted in the frequency of the cases or the intensity of the disease. But these differences which will be indicated when we come to speak of the particular varieties of the epidemic, are sufficiently marked to enable us to account for the general physiological difference between these two epidemics.

By *form* I mean what pathologists were in the habit of designating as varieties. A form is, therefore, not characterised by a single symptom, but by an essential change in the combination and order of succession of the morbid phenomena.†

The cholera disease presents itself under the following four forms:

1. Cholerine.
2. Simple cholera.
3. Ataxic cholera.

---

* See Boerhaave's *Institutiones medicæ*, Paris, 1774, p. 401.

† This does not seem an appropriate place of entering largely upon a discussion of this general pathological question; I have said enough for every enlightened reader.

4. Black or galloping cholera.

I do not consider such general symptoms as an undefinable malaise, lassitude, more or less painful embarrassments of the bowels, and slight attacks of dyspepsia, which many individuals experience during an attack of cholera, as belonging to the disease. I shall simply point out the phenomena which belong to every epidemic, and which proceed in a measure from fear, chagrin, a pre-occupied state of mind, a change in diet and general habits, and from the precautionary measures which had been taken with more or less discretion against the disease.

CHOLERINE.

We frequently designate by this name the diarrhœa that precedes an attack of cholera. By cholerine we here mean the real cholera, also termed cholera diarrhœica, which is the least dangerous variety of the disease.

This form presents itself with various modifications.

Sometimes the accompanying symptoms are so slight, that one hesitates, but improperly, in our judgment, to consider the disease an attack of cholera. These symptoms are a malaise, a sense of soreness and weariness, accompanied by a diarrhœa which is at times a mere serous discharge without colic, and at times a slightly dysenteric attack with acute colic and some nausea. After having lasted from one to three days, this condition disappears of itself, leaving behind it a more or less painful torpor of the digestive canal, which either ceases in a few days, or else continues for several weeks and even months.

In another degree of cholerine we notice either a sudden or else slow and progressive invasion of a serous diarrhœa, which is at first colored and afterwards whitish, accompanied by a general sense of weariness, slight shudderings, followed by nausea and some slight vomiting, after which the sense of general coldness and weakness becomes more marked; at this period some slight cramps are experienced in some part of the body, sometimes in the trunk, and at others in the extremities. This condition is generally transitory. A remission of the symptoms soon takes place, the colic and diarrhœa decrease, the vomiting ceases, the general temperature is restored, accompanied by a slight febrile motion of a day's or half a week's duration. The cramps generally disappear together with the nausea and vomiting; at other times they continue, the patient experiences them several times in the course of twenty-four hours, or else a continuous and dull pain or a weakness, which remains unchanged for a long time, takes their place in the region where the cramps were experienced. The least error in diet may bring back all these accidents, even after they had completely disappeared. A relapse may likewise set in in consequence of great bodily exertions, exposure to the cold air, an excessive repast, violent emotions. In such a case it is a more serious form of cholera that attacks the debilitated constitution. A relapse in this form of cholerine should be represented to the patients as something very dangerous.

Another modification of cholerine consists in a derangement of the digestive functions and organs, accompanied with a moderate febrile motion. The coldness is only felt at the beginning of the disease, when bilious vomiting takes place, together with the bilious or serous diarrhœa, which constitutes a feature in this modification. The head is heavy and painful, the face is more or less flushed, the eyes are slightly injected; the buccal cavity presents symptoms of a congestive irritation, and even of an inflammation, which is characterized by the swelling and redness of the free margin of the gums, the soft deposits on their convex surface, the redness of the tongue at its edges, the thick coating which covers its dorsal surface with more or less uniformity or irregularity, the dryness of the throat, and an intense thirst; the epigastrium is sensitive and feels painful when pressed upon; considerable heat is felt in the region of the stomach, which sometimes extends as high up as under the sternum; in the abdomen the patient complains of seated pains around the navel, or of shifting pains in the hypogastrium or in the sides; the urine is scanty, turbid, and the discharges are not frequent. Cramps occur but seldom; but the soreness, weariness and pains in the extremities are habitual symptoms.

This condition generally lasts seven days; in some cases, however, the malady terminates critically by sweat, nosebleed, abundant or cloudy urine, an erythematous eruption on the skin; generally the malady disappears gradually, leaving behind it, for a shorter or longer period, consecutive phenomena, such as a troublesome stomacace; painfulness of the stomach and dyspepsia; distention and torpor of the bowels, or an irregular diarrhœa; either of these symptoms may occur when the patient exposes himself to the cold, or commits the least error in diet.

Cholerine, which is almost always cured in young people, very often terminates fatally in old persons; they sink gradually, and die after a series of slight relapses. In such cases the intestinal inflammations are generally accompanied by prostration and a comatose drowsiness.

SIMPLE CHOLERA.

This form is generally considered typical of epidemic cholera. I have seen many instances of it towards the close of summer, between the two epidemics of 1832 and 1849. Sauvages asserts, that in his time, some twenty cases of it were admitted every year into his hospital of St. Eloi of Montpellier, if I am not mistaken. This is, proportionally, a much larger number than occurs at Paris, when the disease is not epidemic.

The simple cholera presents two well-marked periods: a frigid period, and a period of reaction, when a cure is about to take place, or else a period of collapse, when the disease terminates fatally. For the sake of more completeness we will divide the phases of the disease into a greater number of periods.

Period of the precursory Symptoms.—The precursory symptoms vary. Sometimes they consist in a diarrhœa without colic, with increasing alvine discharges first of fœcal matter, afterwards of a watery substance which is green or of a pale color, and finally assumes a whitish appearance. This phenomenon may be accompanied by others, but it is sometimes isolated until the actual invasion of the disease. The diarrhœa may be accompanied by colic, with an urging to stool as often as the colic is felt. In such a case the patient generally experiences an increasing feeling of weakness. In other cases the precursory symptoms consist of more general, and more vague phenomena; the head is slightly embarrassed; slight attacks of vertigo take place every now and then; sleep is disturbed; the patient is tormented by an undefinable uneasiness. There is loss of appetite, anorexia, with or without thirst, a bitter or flat taste in the mouth, slight nausea, a certain fulness in the epigastrium, and a sensation as if the hypochondria were traversed by a bar that now rises and then descends again; the abdomen is distended; the patient is seized with urging to stool, after which the diarrhœa develops itself, consisting nearly of profuse serous discharges without any fœcal odor. The patient complains alternately of heat and cold; his face is pale, his complexion sometimes sallow, he looks sad and his voice is somewhat hoarse and thinner. These phenomena increase and decrease alternately. The nausea which accompanies the alvine evacuations, increases more and more; and the nausea is accompanied by weakness, vertigo and coldness until the moment when the disease breaks forth.

If the precursory symptoms do not exist in every case, the cases where they are wanting, are, at any rate, very few. The duration of the precursory period varies from a few hours to several days. During this period most of the patients attend to their business or pleasures. It is sometimes after a meal that the second period commences.

Period of invasion.—This period has three principal symptoms, diarrhœa, vomiting and cramps.

After a feeling of anxiety and malaise, the patient is suddenly seized with a copious vomiting of alimentary substances mixed with liquids and the gastric fluid; he feels easier after the vomiting, but he, at the same time, experiences a sense of coldness, which runs through the trunk and extremities; thirst sets in, but the introduction of beverages into the stomach excites fresh and easy vomitings of fluid substances, which look more or less bilious; the vomiting is speedily followed by a light-colored and profuse diarrhœa, accompanied by borborygmi and soon after by sinking of the abdomen. The nausea which exists simultaneously with the diarrhœa, is soon followed in its turn by vomiting. In the bends of the knees, or in the knees, loins, hypochondria, and in the upper and lower limbs, the patient experiences simple pains, or distressing cramps. At this stage the patients generally take to their beds and try to get warm. But their rest is unceasingly disturbed by alvine or gastric evacuations, or by muscular pains, partial shuddering and coldness. The invasion of the disease is sometimes progressive and, except the vomiting, this period cannot be distinguished without difficulty from the preceding one. It sometimes lasts for some hours without any new symptoms supervening. At other times it sets in abruptly, and the disease develops itself at once as soon as it invades the organism. In some cases the diarrhœa ceases for a moment as soon as the vomiting takes place; there are likewise cases where no cramps occur.

On examining the condition of the organs at the time when the first attack takes place, we find a well-marked inflammatory congestion of the gums and tongue; on its dorsal surface the tongue is covered with a uniform, characteristic, white coating, and at its edges and on its inferior surface, it exhibits a red, somewhat livid color, which contrasts very decidedly with the color of the coating. The throat is likewise irritated; the œsophagus is sometimes painful in its whole extent, the epigastrium is painful to pressure, the abdomen is tormented by colic, which spreads from the navel to the neighboring parts. The urine, which had been scanty until then, ceases to flow; the skin of the hands is cool, likewise that of the face. The aspect of the patient is not yet much altered; but when the attack takes place with violence, the features of the patient alter at once.

Period of increase.—This is termed the cold period, on account of the new symptom which is added to the former. After the vomiting a remarkable change takes place in the pulse, which becomes feeble, irregular, intermittent. The temperature of the extremities sinks, first of the lower, then of the upper. The skin of the extremities looks livid; the face changes rapidly; the eyes seem to retreat into their sockets in consequence of the collapse of the cellular tissue; the nose becomes cold, the lips blueish, the general malaise and the anxiety increase; cramps set in after the alvine discharges, which become more and more frequent, and look whitish, are mixed with grey or white flocks resembling the offal of washed meat, or rice that had been boiled too long. The vomiting becomes more and more copious; the patient is no longer relieved by the vomiting as at first; on the contrary, it is preceded and followed by burning at the epigastrium, under the sternum, and by a painful pressure at the epigastrium. The patient is restless, complaining at times of coldness, at others of heat of the extremities; the cramps become much more frequent; the face and extremities exhibit signs of rapidly increasing emaciation; the livid color of these parts changes to a blueish violet color, which becomes more and more marked. The eyes are dull, dry, the nostrils are frequently covered with a dusty substance, the nose is pointed; the blueish parts are covered with a cold sweat; the pulse becomes smaller, feebler, more imperceptible, at times regular, at others unequal and intermittent, or slower or more frequent than in a normal state of the system. The voice becomes gradually extinct, and the patient speaks only in a low tone of voice; and when he does speak, it is only to ask for drink, wherewith to quench his burning thirst. He is also heard to moan or to utter plaintive cries when the violent cramps seize him. The cramps become more and more painful, more and more general. Generally they decrease under the influence of heat and frictions. But all such relief does not last long.

Sometimes the accidents seem to cease for some hours, and it seems as though a real remission of the symptoms were setting in; but soon after, the diarrhœa, the vomiting, cramps, blueness and coldness reappear with an increased intensity. These illusory remissions may last a day or a night; but then the symptoms return with increased violence at the hour when they had broken out the day before. These remissions have given rise to the belief that there is an intermittent cholera.

The period of growth lasts from a few hours to twenty-four and even forty-eight hours, after which the symptoms seem to remain stationary for some time.

Acme.—When the disease has reached its acme, the symptoms remain for some time the same; they present a complete development of the cholera.

The patient generally lies on his back; the position of the patient varies according as he is quiet or restless.

The features of the patient exhibit what is termed the hippocratic face. Its complexion is cyanotic, especially the ears, nose, eyelids, lips; this blueish color invades the upper part of the neck, and sometimes the whole neck. Generally the face is without any expression; nevertheless the sensations and even the feelings of the patient are still depicted in it; it looks frightful when the patient is tormented by cramps.

The skin of the trunk frequently preserves a certain warmth; that of the extremities is cold, livid, blueish, wrinkled, dry or moist. The intellectual faculties are undisturbed, the senses preserve their respective faculties. However, the patient is troubled with vertigo, buzzing in the ears, and does not wish to talk.

The pains are more or less violent and scattered; the most intolerable of the pains are the burning under the sternum, the bar across the epigastrium, and cramps in the muscles of the trunk.

The muscular strength is considerably decreased; nevertheless the patient is still able to sit up in bed either for the purpose of drinking or vomiting; the trunk and the extremities move with an astonishing ease.

The breathing, which is frequently natural, is often embarassed by the constrictive cramp-pains of the thoracic muscles; it is sometimes hurried. The voice has no resonance, or it is hoarse and feeble; at the base of the thorax the patient experiences an anxiety which sometimes increases to a perfect agony, and makes the patient say that he is choking.

The beats of the heart are weaker than in a normal state; the pulse of the large arteries corresponds with the beats of the heart; at the wrist the pulse sometimes differs, being either very small or completely extinct. Sometimes it is only felt on one side.

The tongue and mouth are the seat of a well-marked stomacace; in many cases the throat is similarly affected. The vomiting at this stage may be considered typical of the vomiting in cholera; likewise the atonic discharges. In the discharges from the stomach or bowels, the bile has entirely disappeared. The urinary secretion is completely suppressed; the secretion of tears and nasal mucus likewise ceases. In some patients sweat breaks out, not only on the extremities, but on the trunk also.

Terminations: in death.—After a momentary remission of the symptoms and a slight reappearance of warmth at the extremities and of the radial pulse, this latter becomes frequent, small, imperceptible; the vomitings take place at longer intervals, and the stools become involuntary. The patient is tormented by a desire for sleep, which he is unable to satisfy; he becomes silent, closes his eyelids, remains motionless, except when he is seized with the cramps or the vomiting; the blueish color becomes still darker; it extends above the wrists, where it changes to a livid hue, that gradually spreads over the trunk. A viscid sweat covers the face and extremities; the beats of the heart become weaker, the breathing shorter, hurried, the eyelids are almost motionless, half open; the eye is so dry that the choroïd membrane is almost seen through the sclerotica, and the patient dies after a death-struggle of a few hours.

In recovery.—If the disease terminates in recovery, we have a different group of symptoms. The morbid phenomena disappear gradually in the reverse order of their original development. The symptoms that appeared last, are the first to yield.

The warmth of the extremities returns gradually; the blueness disappears; the eyes become more prominent, the features assume a more pleasant expression. The blueness is gradually replaced by a less livid and brighter color. The pulse begins to beat feebly, but regularly; the cramps become much less frequent; the vomiting becomes easier, less frequent and copious; the evacuations again become bilious, first yellowish, afterwards greenish, and, instead of continuing serous and grumous, they change to evacuations of fœcal matter. The patient desires to urinate, and succeeds in emitting a slight quantity of cloudy urine; the voice becomes stronger; the patient feels better, although he still complains of malaise, headache, heaviness of the head, burning in the chest and stomach.

If the remission continues, the symptoms gradually disappear; the blueness ceases entirely, the coldness is succeeded by a warmth, which is either uniformly mild and equal, or else unequal, slight at the extremities and burning at the trunk. The urine is secreted regularly, the cramps cease, the vomiting becomes less and less; the diarrhœa, which was the first symptom when the disease broke out, is the last to yield. Finally, sleep sets in, and with it a feeling of ease. Recovery is not always as easily accomplished. A more or less intense fever sets in, with congestions of the head, eyes, local inflammations of the mouth, stomach or bowels. All the symptoms may have ceased, and a single one may have remained. Sometimes the cramps remain, at others the bilious vomiting, as effect of a gastritis, or a bilious diarrhœa, from which we infer a bilious inflammation of the bowels; the cerebral congestion sometimes yields with much difficulty. As long as the symptoms have not entirely disappeared, some new disorder frequently shows itself retarding the happy termination of the disease.

The period of reaction is sometimes a deception both to the patient and the physician. *After* a remission of the symptoms, which is always incomplete in such a case, and may last from a few hours to one or two days, the symptoms of the disease suddenly reappear in all their intensity; the cerebral congestions again develop themselves, the breathing becomes shorter, the coldness and blueness again become perceptible, and the patient sinks into the stage of collapse, which is sometimes accompanied by a profound coma, and, at other times, is without any cerebral congestion and without coma.

Genuine cholera generally terminates on the first day, on the third, seventh or fourteenth, from the day of invasion. This termination takes place with or without critical changes, generally without. The most frequent critical changes are sweats, nosebleed, cutaneous eruptions; after these crises there sometimes remains some important secondary phenomenon, such as stomacace, gastritis, enteritis, or muscular pains and weaknesses; these frequently occur in the lower extremities.

Convalescence does not really set in until after the crisis. It lasts more or less long, according to the the age; old people recover slowly and with difficulty, young people on the contrary, recover speedily, easily, and completely. I have never noticed any desquamation of the epidermis or falling off of the hair taking place during this period.

Simple genuine cholera has a number of varieties, especially in regard to the intensity of the disease, which is of several degrees, although always very serious. These various degrees of intensity depend upon the intensity of the symptoms in the cold stage, or upon the affections which develop themselves during the period of reaction. The more or less rapid development of the symptoms of the first period, the decided character of the remission and the setting in of positive convalescence; or the oscillations between the remission and the return of the phenomena of the period of increase; the duration of the period of reaction; the difficulty of restoring the functions, and lastly, the secondary phenomena: all these various conditions constitute important differences.

This form of the disease prevailed principally at the commencement of the epidemic of 1849. This was not the case in 1832. Although many cases occurred during the first period of the epidemic, nevertheless, the black or galloping form of the disease was much more frequent than during the second epidemic. This accounts for the difference in the mortality of the commencement of the two epidemics. With a few exceptions the first hundred cases all terminated fatally in the various wards of the Hotel Dieu. In 1849, on the contrary, the mortality was proportionately less at the commencement than during the progress of the epidemic. The cause of this was, that there were more cases of simple cholera at the beginning, than towards the middle of the epidemic. This form of the disease is much less fatal than either of the two forms, of which we shall now proceed to give a description.

Ataxic form.—Like the former variety, so has this one precursory symptoms; but I am not prepared to assert that these symptoms have anything characteristic. It has three well-marked periods, an irregular cold period, a period of incomplete remission, and a typhoid period. The frequency of this form in the epidemic of 1849 seems to have constituted one of its peculiar features. It was very scarce in 1832. Let us proceed to a description of its progressive development.

Cold Period.—This period commences and develops itself to all appearance as the period of increase in simple cholera. An attentive observer, however, may discover differences which are sometimes very striking and at other times very doubtful. Thus, the patients show from the commencement a prostration of strength which is not at all proportionate to the other symptoms. The discharges may be very slight and the weakness may nevertheless have reached a high degree of development. On the other hand, excessive evacuations from the stomach and bowels take place without either cramps or cyanosis being present. Or the face may have assumed a slightly blueish tint, and the pulse be entirely gone at the wrist; and, on the other hand, the pulse may still exist, with feeble, frequent, unequal and irregular beats, whereas the cyanosis of the face and extremities is already fully developed. As regards the temperature of the body, it is likewise very irregular: the lower extremities may be cold, whilst the upper extremities are warm, and vice-versa. The discharges may be moderate, whilst all the other symptoms are strikingly developed, the face and extremities are of a violet-color, and the pulse is imperceptible. Generally, the patients are either very restless, or very drowsy, and dislike to be roused. These are the principal irregularities which distinguish the cold period of ataxic cholera. They do not, by any means, exist together in the same individual. In some cases only one of these irregularities exists, in others several; in some again they are found united. In the former case it is almost impossible to distinguish, at this period, ataxic cholera from the simple form, which has many varieties. The cold period generally lasts from six to twelve hours, and sometimes longer.

Period of incomplete remission.—I have scarcely ever seen it wanting entirely, but it is more or less marked. What distinguishes it from the period of remission in the simple cholera, is this that the symptoms do not disappear in the reverse order of their original development. The blueness may disappear, and yet the warmth not return. The pulse which had ceased to beat, may become perceptible without the cyanosis disappearing; and the cyanosis and coldness may have given place to a natural color and temperature, whereas the evacuations are much more copious and frequent. The vomiting and the alvine evacuations may cease, and yet the strength, the warmth or the pulse may not return. The patient may be talkative, restless; he may not feel thirsty, or he may experience a fainting sensation in the epigastrium, which seems to him like hunger. In some cases the cramps are violent and extremely painful, in other cases they are scarcely perceptible, some patients keep their voice almost entirely. This period may last a few moments only, or two and even three days, it is always followed by the third period which we shall proceed to describe.

Typhoid stage.—This period sets in with drowsiness or delirium. But in proportion as the cerebral phenomena develop themselves more strikingly, we behold, in the place of a febrile reaction proportionate to the cerebral irritation, a marked development of cyanosis and coldness. Nothing is more remarkable, more characteristic than these cold inflammations which develop themselves in the typhoid stage of ataxic cholera; this is the highest degree of the malignant form of the disease. In some cases, the bronchia, the stomach or bowels are the seat of well-marked congestions or inflammations, without any diminution of the cyanosis or coldness. Generally the pulse remains perceptible, except during the death-struggle, which is almost always protracted, slow, accompanied with coma, and very frequently with a stertorous, noisy respiration.

Whereas, in simple cholera, the local irritations of the period of reaction set in with a marked febrile excitement, they are accompanied in the ataxic form of cholera with coldness and cyanosis. It seems scarcely necessary to point out this difference.

The ataxic form is deceptive; at first it seems less serious than simple cholera; its symptoms are less united, and some of the ordinary cholera-symptoms are even wanting; but the spurious and incomplete remission which develops itself in the second stage, soon disturbs the physician; nevertheless he may remain deceived even then. The third stage can only deceive those who wish to be deceived.

Galoping or black Cholera.—So far as a description of its symptoms is concerned, this variety is the simplest of any. Generally it has a precursory stage; but it does not always last any length of time, only a few hours; in some cases the precursory symptoms are entirely wanting. The diarrhœa, vomiting, blueness, coldness, and cramps set in all together. The patient may be struck during his sleep, at table or while taking a walk. It even happens that he is unable to rise from the chair on which he had seated himself to support his bowels; sometimes he suddenly falls down in a swoon; the voice becomes extinct, the features are altered; the color of the face and that of the extremities change visibly, and the blueness gradually spreads over the whole body. After the attack has commenced, the patient is not allowed any rest; the discharges and cramps succeed each other without interruption; the pulse disappears, the secretions stop, the cadaverous aspect becomes more and more marked. Life frequently ceases all at once in the midst of the cramps and discharges that have become involuntary; or the patient may sink into a collapse of some hours, during which the mind and the muscular movements become progressively weaker, whilst the whole body turns black, becomes icy-cold, covered with a clammy sweat and looks truly frightful. This variety lasts from two to twenty hours.

Having analysed the phenomena of cholera through their order of succession and combination, and having, in this way, given the history of the different varieties of this epidemic, we might now study each separate symptom and lesion, and study their modifications in regard to form, degree and period, for the purpose of arriving at a proper appreciation of the diagnostic and prognostic value of each symptom; but howsoever useful and necessary to a complete picture of the cholera-disease this might be, such an undertaking would carry us too far away from the end that we have proposed to ourselves, namely: the application of Hahnemann's method to the treatment of this disease. We have been obliged to limit ourselves to what has seemed to us indispensable.

Moreover the therapeutic analysis will, in a measure, replace the semeiotic portion; we will therefore pass over at once to the principal object of our investigations.

§ III. THERAPEUTIC ANALYSIS.

The preceding chapters have, it seems to me, sufficiently established the fact, that the physiology and pathology of cholera are as well known as those of any other severe disease. It remains to be shown, that the treatment of cholera can be conducted upon a truly scientific basis. This does not mean that such a treatment must prove efficacious in every case; the facts would contradict any such assumption. All we mean to affirm, is, that the indications and corresponding curative means in cholera can be scientifically shown; that the successes or failures in the treatment of cholera can be accounted for; and that what has been done and what yet remains to be done in this matter, can be accurately determined.

Let us commence with the facts; afterwards we will explain the method.

By facts we mean a description of the first twenty

cases which came into our ward in the epidemic of 1849. Of the cases which arrived afterwards, we simply took a few notes. It would have been impossible, at a time when the increase of the epidemic brought to our hospital an increasing number of patients, to conciliate the duties of our office with the time required by elaborate statements of the cases. These twenty cases will be, moreover, found sufficient to enable us to substantiate our inferences.

We shall give the cases in the order in which the patients were brought to the hospital; and we shall accompany each case with such remarks concerning its nosography or therapeutics, as may seem requisite to place its most striking features in a stronger light. It should not be forgotten that the description which we have given of cholera, is not taken from these twenty cases, but that it results from the study of the two epidemics of 1832 and 1849.

CASE. I.—By Dr. Guyton.—*Epidemic Cholera; variety: simple Cholera.—Cure.*

Séfert, 58 years, carpenter, was brought to the hospital on the 29th of March, 1849, ward St. Benjamin, No. 10, (hospital Sainte Marguérite.)

The patient seemed to have a good constitution, and looked robust. Six days previous to being taken with cholera, he had been attacked with a diarrhœa that was sufficiently violent to compel him to quit work on account of the frequency of the evacuations. They did not make him very sick, however. Having become impatient, Séfert concluded to stop his diarrhœa by a violent remedy, and got drunk. About midnight he returned home, went to bed, but the next morning he was so weak that he was unable to dress himself, and laid down again. About noon a relative who came to see him, and who got frightened by the vomiting, the diarrhœa, and the altered features of the patient, had him carried to the hospital.

One o'clock.—The patient showed the following symptoms: marked cholera physiognomy, eyes sunken, nose pointed, malar bones very prominent, features shrunk.

Tongue moist, whitish, cold; pain at the epigastrium, sensation as if a bar were stretched across; loathing, frequent nausea; ardent thirst; abdomen flat, not painful to pressure, except at the epigastric region. Immediately after entering the hospital, the patient was seized with copious vomiting of a clear watery substance which had a slightly greenish tinge. During my visit at half past two, the patient had four successive vomitings of the same substance.

The breathing was a little shorter and more frequent than in a normal condition; no aphonia, pulse very small, filiform, almost imperceptible; marked blueness of the fingers, hands; some of the veins of the forearms were swollen, blue, and very prominent on the skin.

Coldness of the tongue, face, the whole surface of the body, and more particularly of the extremities; frequent cramps in the calves, insteps, hands; they are very painful. Complete suppression of the urinary secretion; percussion showed that the bladder was empty. Prostration. Mind unimpaired; the patient's answers are not always very clear, and he waits some time before speaking.

Took *Carbo-veget.* 6, a small tablespoonful every hour, and on account of the feeling of loathing and the sickness at the stomach, *Bryonia* 3, every ten minutes; warm blankets.

At four o'clock, two stools of a sickly smelling substance, having a whitish-grey color, and resembling perfectly a decoction of rice, several grains of which had split open, and were crushed.

At five o'clock, took *Nux-vomica* 3, a spoonful every

ten minutes, for the desire to vomit, instead of the Bryonia, that did not seem to have produced any effect.

Half past seven. Same general appearance. The patient has warmed up, about the head and trunk, even on the feet, but the warmth is not regularly distributed. He complains of internal heat. The pulse is stronger, more frequent, but continues very soft and compressible. The blueness has disappeared; there are only some traces of it under the nails. Respiration short, frequent; sound of the voice rather false, hoarse. Tongue moist; intense thirst. No stool; two other attacks of vomiting; abdomen sunken in, not painful to pressure, except in the epigastric region, where pressure excites an acute pain, that makes the patient to distort his features. These pains in the stomach, however, are spontaneous; they constitute a rest of painful compression; some slight paroxysms of cough increase them. Cramps in the legs and fingers are a little less frequent; the motions of the hands are yet beyond the control of the will. Headache, but no tightness or cramps. Gave *Arsenic* 6, in solution, on account of the sensation of internal heat. Afterwards a solution of *Carbo-veg*. 24. No urine, skin dry.

March 30.—The face looks about the same. The tongue is moist, but continues colder than in the normal state. Breathing hurried, but longer. Pulse a little fuller but soft and compressible, 60 per minute. Skin tolerably warm, dry. Abdomen depressed, painful in the epigastric region. Shifting cramps. No vomiting during the night, the patient has slept a little at various times. This morning a stool of middling quantity, but of a different character, of a uniform yellow color, some consistence, resembling a bilious diarrhœa of fair appearance. Passed a small quantity of urine. The patient complains of acute seated pains in the knees.

Carbo-veg. 24, and *China* 12, both in solution, for the pain in the knees.

Four o'clock in the evening. Two attacks of vomiting of a leek-colored substance, bilious, perfectly characteristic, of middling quantity. Tongue moist, whitish, still a little cold. The expression of the face is somewhat improved, the features are less shrunk, the eyes still sunken, and dry. Skin warm, dry, pungent heat on the abdomen, and in various other circumscribed places. The bowels are depressed, the pain at the epigastric region still continues. No stool, or emission of urine. Pulse 64; dull headache.

March 31.—Expression of the face improved, intelligent; the eyes are less sunken, more animated; the region of the cheek-bone is dark-colored. Tongue moist, of a normal temperature, covered with a whitish coating, the edges and the tip somewhat red; gums red with a whitish border (slight stomacace). The heat of the body is milder, uniform, of the common temperature of the breath; the pulse is fuller, firmer, 64. No pain at the abdomen or epigastrium from pressure. The patient coughs now and then; he sneezes freely. No cramps; the pain in the knees continues. Calm sleep in the night, and of some length at times. No headache, no vomiting, no stool, one emission of urine. Breathing longer, quieter, the voice has a more natural sound.

The general appearance of the patient is much better, the mind clear; there remains some uneasiness and restlessness in the manner, gestures, speech and looks of the patient.

Carbo-veget. in solution: wine of Bagnolles.

Evening: Mild, even, respiratory warmth; moist skin; eyes moist, full of tears; breathing easy, several quiet naps in the day-time. No headache, or pain at the stomach; no vomiting or stool. The patient passed urine three times in considerable quantity, and without any difficulty. No pain any where, except in the knees. Pulse 60, regular, firm; the patient feels much better, he wants to eat. Broth and wine.

April 1st.--Is getting better all the time. Sound sleep, normal temperature, no pain, pulse 60, urinary secretion perfectly restored, good appetite. Broths and soups. The pain in the knees continues. *China* 12 in solution.

April 2d.—Complete convalescence. Last night had a papescent stool, of a natural color and smell. Urinary secretion, pulse, breathing, temperature all natural, return of strength, knees free from pain, has some more flying pains in the legs.

China in solution. One tumblerful.

In the day-time the patient takes a walk in the garden.

April 3d.—The pains have ceased; the treatment is stopped. The convalescence went on without any interruption; on the 7th of April the patient's health was perfectly restored; on the 11th he was discharged cured.

This case is an example of what we have termed simple or genuine cholera. It was a severe case, without, however, presenting any very intense symptoms. We took a lively interest in this case; it was the first case of cholera treated homœopathically in our hospital.

At the commencement of the treatment we hesitated a little between Bryonia and Nux-vomica. Nux effected an improvement. However, it having been given together with the charcoal, it might be difficult to determine the part that each remedy had in this result. Arsenic was substituted for Nux, and since then, the cure advanced slowly but perceptibly.

On the third day the disease seemed broken, and the patient's convalescence beyond all doubt. The only obstacle in the way was the continuance of the pain in the knees and legs. Consequently the period which we have termed the period of reaction, was a real remission.

CASE II.—By Dr. Guyton.—*Epidemic Cholera; galoping or black Cholera.—Death.*

Ward St. Benjamin, No. 1.

Regeret, 62 years old, basket-maker. Brought to the hospital at 6 o'clock in the evening.

Yesterday and this morning the patient enjoyed good health; he worked as usual until 9 o'clock in the morning; suddenly he was attacked with diarrhœa and copious vomiting. Intense thirst; pain in the back, cramps; quite cold.

He was brought to the hospital in the following state: Cadaverous physiognomy, in the full sense of the term; eyes deeply sunken; face shrunk, livid, cold as marble; tongue white, moist, cold; intense thirst. No pulse; general cyanosis; the extremities almost black. Quite cold all over.

Breathing short, superficial, frequent; complete loss of voice.

The abdomen is sunken; the epigastrium painful; sensation of cramps at the stomach. Liquid vomiting after entering, clear as water, with a slight greenish tinge.

Understanding perfectly lucid, muscular strength pretty fair; painful and frequent cramps in the calves and toes.

Solution of *Veratrum* 3.—Application of warm clothes. —Water sweetened with sugar.

From 9 o'clock until midnight the patient warmed up over the lower half of his body; the upper portion of the trunk, the neck and face are covered with a cold, clammy sweat, collecting in drops here and there. These parts become likewise more livid; the skin loses its elasticity. The features become more and more altered, the eyes sink, become dull, lose their expression; the eyelids are depressed. Acute cramps in the legs. Constant pains at the stomach; no more vomiting; three bright, yellowish stools. The breathing is frequent and feebler. No pulse. Auscultation scarcely reveals a tremulous motion in the region of heart, indicating the contractions of this organ, and partially obscured by the respiratory murmur.

I left the patient at two in the morning, I had expected for some time to see him die every minute.

April 3d.—The patient is still alive, but in great agony, the understanding perfectly clear; the cadaverous appearance becomes more and more marked. Pulse scarcely perceptible. The skin on the chest has warmed up a little under the influence of the warm clothes; but it seems a superficial heat. No reaction; the skin has taken up a little of the warmth of the surrounding objects. It continues covered with a viscous sweat that seems rather warm, but leaves a sensation of coldness.

Tongue cold, intense thirst. Yellow-watery stool, uniformly colored, not grumous. Liquid and clear vomiting, with a slightly greenish tinge.

Voice gone. The animal strength is not quite prostrated; the patient sits up in his bed, turns about. Painful cramps in the feet.

Two attacks of vomiting in the day-time; another stool.

About three o'clock, the patient who had been gradually sinking since morning, becomes listless, ceases to answer questions, the breathing becomes shorter and shorter, and he dies at 6 o'clock.

At the morning-visit, the patient had been ordered to take *Arsenic* and *Carbo-veg.* 6, in solution, every five minutes, alternately.

There never was a sign of reaction, no pulse. The patient looked like a speaking and feeling corpse; it was a condition that defies description.

Autopsy: Right ventricle, and the large veins filled with black, coagulated blood; the abdominal veins full of blood. Viscera empty. Peyer's glands greyish, perfectly perceptible, somewhat prominent. Scattered red spots in the bowels.

Bladder empty.

No morbid signs in the brain.

This case of black cholera set in at once, without any precursory symptoms, with all the intensity of the disease. The cyanosis was general. There was no reaction. Is the prolonged agony to be attributable to the treatment? This seems indeed all that it accomplished.

CASE III.—By Dr. Guyton.—*Epidemic Cholera; simple Cholera.—Cure.*

Ward St. Benjamin, No. 35.

Durand, 37 years, gardener, brought to the hospital on the 7th, when the visits were taking place.

For five days past, has had diarrhœa, loss of appetite. In the night from the 6th to the 7th the patient is suddenly attacked with vomiting and diarrhœa, the discharges being very frequent. On entering the hospital, the patient showed the following symptoms:

Characteristic cholera-face; marked lividity, especially at the tip of the nose, round the mouth, and on the chin. Eyes sunken, blueish circle round the orbit; respiration frequent, much shorter than in health; voice feeble, husky; pulse small, soft, disappearing under the slightest pressure, and sometimes ceasing for a time. Cyanosis, especially at the above-mentioned parts. The fingers, back, hands are livid; the skin is shrivelled.

General coldness, especially of the extremities, face, neck, tongue, extremities; skin dry.

Tongue moist, slightly whitish, cold; abdomen depressed, painful to pressure, the epigastric and umbilical regions are painful without any pressure being made; these pains are acute. Thirst intense. The Patient has had many attacks of easy vomiting during the night; the liquid is projected in one stream; it is white, watery containing a small quantity of mucus that contrasts with the transparent fluid. Stools liquid, copious, resembling a decoction of crushed rice, white, having a sickly smell, and expelled without trouble.

Urinary secretion suspended; bladder empty.

The understanding is perfectly clear; the patient answers questions promptly and correctly; he seems resigned and submissive; the strength is natural, the patient turns about in his bed, helps himself; has some cramps in the lower extremities.

We have then diarrhœa in the precursory stage, and afterwards sudden invasion of severe cholera. A general examination of the case shows that the patient is very sick.

All the symptoms are well marked. The preservation of the pulse, however, although it is very feeble, is a good sign. The frequent vomiting (several attacks occurring during the visit), and the peculiar pain at the stomach point to *Veratrum* 3, and *Carbo-veget.* 6, in alternation every five minutes, and, towards evening, every ten minutes.—Warm cloths; water sweetened with sugar for drink.

Eight o'clock in the evening.—The patient who had been closely watched all day, has warmed up after a few hours' treatment. The warmth is mild, of a good quality, without sweat. The patient has had several attacks of vomiting in the afternoon; towards four o'clock the vomiting is much less frequent and less copious, one or two mouthfuls each time. Three characteristic stools, liquid as mentioned above, including the morning-evacuation. The last stool is less copious, and more consistent than the other two.

The face has a better expression; the tongue is warmer. Voice, respiration, condition of the abdomen, as above. Pulse fuller, stronger, less frequent; a few cramps; no urine.

April 8th.—The patient has had several naps during the night. Two or three attacks of slight vomiting, before 10 o'clock. During the night, three stools: the first a little more consistent than the former evacuations, liquid but with a greenish tinge; the second stool less copious, still more consistent and greener; the third still more consistent, of a strong greenish-yellow color. There was a marked progression from the liquid to the physiological normal form in these evacuations; every successive stool contained a larger proportion of intestinal mucus and biliary matter. This morning an attack of vomiting half clear, half leek-colored.

Temperature good, pulse full, tongue warm. The cyanosis of the face and hands disappears, physiognomy improved. Pain in the bowels less; some nausea. Cramps subdued; no urine. *Carbo-veget.* 6, *Ipecac.* 12, in solution, every hour alternately, in tablespoonful doses.

In the day-time a stool similar to the above.

April 9.—Improved expression of countenance, quiet features. The lividity has disappeared, the eyes look natural; no cyanosis. Uniform mild warmth all over no sweat. Pulse regular, of normal frequency, soft but not feeble. Breathing good; the voice has recovered its sound and vigor. Abdominal pains less; no vomiting; scanty stool; three discharges of urine in the morning. Little thirst; sound sleep; good night's rest. *Carbo-veget.* 6, in solution.

Evening.—Papescent very green stool; three easy discharges of urine, copious in the afternoon.

April 10th.—Convalescence perfectly evident; refreshing sleep; mild warmth of the skin, like the temperature of the breath; pulse normal. No pain. Two stools since last evening: the first thick and green; the second green and in form. Normal discharge of urine.

Tongue looks natural, appetite and thirst natural.

Two platefuls of broth; water with wine and sugar. *Carbo-veget.* as above.

Evening.—Craving appetite; abdomen of natural distention, no pain.

April 11th.—Complete convalescence. During the day an eruption like nettle-rash breaks out on the abdomen, lower extremities, back and arms. Inconvenient itching.

A meal; no medicine.

April 12th.—The eruption continues, no other abnormal symptoms. Appetite. The patient rises.

April 13th.—Eruption the same.

„ 14th.—The eruption disappears.

„ 15th.—The patient is discharged cured.

This case seems remarkable both for the regularity of the cholera-phenomena and for the efficacy of the treatment. A theoretical difficulty, however, presents itself. What part in the cure have the charcoal and the white Hellebore respectively? they were administered conjointly first every five, and then every ten minutes in alternation. The simplicity of the phenomena during the reaction, and the ease with which recovery took place after such a well-marked cold period, are striking.

CASE IV.—*by Dr. Guyton.—Epidemic Cholera; galoping or black Cholera.—Death.*

Féret, forty years old, nail maker, was brought to the hospital on the seventh of April, 1849, at seven o'clock in the evening. Ward St. Benjamin No. 37.

The patient was very small, awfully rickety and deformed; he had a most sickly appearance. Was habitually moderate in his diet, but lived in an unhealthy house, on unwholesome food.

At nine in the morning, the patient had taken his breakfast; no abnormal symptom existed previous to this moment. After the meal he was suddenly taken with diarrhœa and vomiting, the paroxysms succeeding each other in uninterrupted succession.

Record of symptoms: Cadaverous face; eyes sunken, surrounded with a blueish circle; livid color round the lips, wings of the nose. Breathing rather full and quiet; voice extinct, only a breath. Pulse very weak, stopping at times, pretty regular, but more frequent than in health. The beats of the heart are easily heard. Marked cyanosis of the face, fingers, the dorsal surfaces of the hands and feet. Intense coldness of the face, neck, upper and lower extremeties; skin dry, cadaverous, without elasticity. Tongue moist, somewhat coated white, cold; painfulness of the abdomen, when pressed upon, or even without pressure; the abdomen is depressed, drawn-in, sinking, so to say, under the prominence of the deformed thorax. Frequent vomitings and stools in the day-time; immediately after entering the hospital the patient vomited up a clear liquid mixed with a little green matter, that falls to the bottom of the vessel. The alvine evacuations pass off against the will of the patient; he is scarcely conscious of their passage. Intense thirst; the urinary secretion is suspended; no urine in the bladder. Understanding clear; nevertheless the patient, who is prostrated and lying on the back, looks rather stupid; he closes his eyes, has to be urged to answer questions, answers by signs or in a tone of voice that is scarcely intelligible, and without opening his eyes. He thinks he is past cure. Painful cramps in the lower limbs; they occur frequently; the patient expresses his pain by moaning and distortion of the features.

The distressing appearance of this patient can scarcely be described. He is deeply struck; the prognosis suggested by these symptoms, is exceedingly doubtful. During the last moments of our examination the patient sinks more and more into this painful torpor, which we have described; a cold sweat breaks out on the face and neck; these parts become icy-cold and feel sticky. The pulse is collapsing, and life seems on the point of departing.

Warm cloths. *Carbo-veg*. 6, and *Arsenicum* 6, both in solution, a tablespoonful of each, alternately, every five minutes.

At ten o'clock in the evening, the whole chest, face and upper extremities were covered with a cold and viscid sweat; the lower extremities were cold as ice. Only the abdomen felt a little warm. The pulse had entirely disappeared. The trunk was cyanosed; the hands had a dark and livid appearance; on pinching up the skin, it remained so. The anguish was excessive. Painful cramps were experienced every moment, and caused the patient to moan. He vomited, and passed stool without knowing it. About midnight the agony had reached its climax; he died at half past one in the morning.

There was no post-mortem examination.

(Recorded by Dr. Guyton.)

This case shows that in the last stage of black cholera, the treatment is inefficacious.

In this as in the former case of black cholera, there were no precursory symptoms.

CASE V.—*Epidemic Cholera; ataxic variety; a cure.*

Balagnat, 38 years old, cabinetmaker, brought to the hospital on the 13th of April, at half past seven in the morning. Ward St. Benjamin, No. 3.

The patient had worked at his trade the whole of the previous day, without experiencing any unpleasant feeling; his health was good. In the middle of the night he was taken with frequent vomiting and diarrhœa; cramps set in at 5 in the morning.

Record: Face emaciated, features elongated, eyes

deeply sunken. Extremely sad expression of countenance; the patient is very uneasy about his condition.

Respiration normal as regards frequency, or extension, voice feeble and as if hoarse. Pulse well marked, regular, hard, frequent, 120. The malar, region, the region around the mouth and eyes are livid, lips violet-colored, lower face and tongue blueish. The whole thorax, neck, hands and forearms are livid. Cyanosis of the lower extremities; a network of numerous veins, engorged and raised on the skin, without circulation, is visible on the insteps, legs, thighs. Upon entering the hospital, the patient's skin was rather cool than cold, as it usually is, some time after having been lying down, the heat of the skin is restored; it was quite striking. At the same time a hot sweat breaks out in the face, on the neck, chest, arms. The pulse was very full.

Tongue coated white on the upper surface; moist, rather cool. Thirst intense, pains in the epigastrium very acute, like cramps, not much aggravated by pressure. Abdomen depressed, not painful. Scanty vomiting during the visit; shortly after, three or four other attacks of vomiting of a clear liquid like water, with a greenish tinge. Copious stool after the visit; a yellowish liquid without clots. No secretion of urine.

Mind clear, but spirits depressed, discouraged. Good amount of physical strength, the patient turns about in his bed with much firmness of will, helps himself. Uninterrupted and painful cramps in the hands and especially in the calves; the patient complains of them very bitterly, this symptom troubles him more than any other.

The disease sets in without any precursory symptoms. Prognosis unfavorable; there does not seem to be any regularity in the symptoms of the disease. For instance, a marked cyanosis, and a stoppage of the capillary circulation and even of the circulation of the veins of a certain size, co-exist with a certain force and even hardness of the pulse, warmth of the skin, and warm sweat.

Water sweetened with sugar of the ordinary temperature. *Veratrum* 3 in solution. Warm cloths.

Evening.—Second visit three hours after the former. The vomiting has ceased; the patient complains a good deal of his cramps. Was ordered a solution of two drops of the spirits of camphor. At 8 o'clock, the pulse is down to 100, the cramps have ceased; the muscular pains are much less.

At 11 o'clock the temperature of the skin is milder, the sweating has ceased. Pulse softer, down to 88. General improvement.

Carbo-veget. 6, and the aforesaid solution of Camphor, alternately every half hour.

April 14th, second day.—Several calm naps during the night. Respiration regular, voice firmer. Pulse more natural, down to 80. The cyanosis is less, the veins of the extremities are less swollen, the circulation recommences. The hands, chest, neck and especially the face are less livid. The warmth is of good quality, but not uniform, no sweat.

Tongue moist, rather cool. Two scanty vomitings this morning, clear as water. The pain in the epigastrium is much less; the patient complains rather of a sensation of malaise and weakness. A stool in the night, of more consistence and darker color, slightly green. A scanty discharge of urine in the morning.

The patient continues very sad, the depression of spirits remains the same. Some not very painful cramps at long intervals.

Carbo-veget. 6, and Camphor in solution as above. A few spoonfuls of broth.

Evening.—No stool since. Two watery vomitings after having tasted a little broth; was not given any more. Some nausea. Warm skin; face pretty full;

slight restlessness. Pulse full, 76. Same signs of cyanosis. No more cramps. Depression of spirits continues.

Carbo-veget. without the Camphor.

Evening, 11 o'clock.—Watery vomiting mixed with mucous flocks. No stool.

April 15th, third day.—Sleep during the night. Vomits twice in the morning; has a grey-colored stool with clots.

No more cyanosis. Pulse full, large, 80. Skin pretty hot, face red, no sweat. The febrile phenomena have been very marked from the first. Abdomen flat, not painful. Intense thirst.

Nux-vomica 12 in solution.

Evening.—Vomiting with a pretty thick yellowish-green deposit. Nausea.

Same solution.

April 16th, fourth day.—Warmth milder, more natural, uniform; better pulse. No pain, the patient only complains of weakness. No vomiting; yellow stool of pretty fair appearance. Two discharges of urine. Less thirst.

Continue the Nux-vomica at intervals of two hours.

Evening.—Yellow stool of a very good color, with thick, almost solid fæces.

April 17, fifth day.—The patient feels pretty comfortable. Three bilious stools composed of solid fæces that look sound and of natural weight. No vomiting or nausea.

Gentle warmth of the skin, pulse quiet and easy. The face recovers its natural expression and color.

Appetite: broth. Continue the *Nux.*

Evening.—No stool during the day.

April 18, sixth day.—Two stools composed of papescent fæccs.

Gentle warmth, like the breath, pulse quiet. Breathing full and easy, the voice has a good sound. Still some weakness, the secretions are restored.

Appetite: lean soups. Wine of Bagnolles.

April 19 and 20.—Progressive improvement.

April 21.—The patient is quite well; his spirits are good, except a remaining touch of melancholy.

This morning the skin feels a little hot; slight stomacace, the tongue is covered with a thick yellowish mucus, the edges are red and the papillæ elevated. Gums red with a greyish border round the teeth.

No stool. The patient walks about the room.

Aconite 12 in solution. Soups.

April 22.—Complete convalescence.

" 23.—The stomacace has ceased.

Discharged cured on the 30th of April.

This case is interesting in many respects; who, for instance, would not be struck by the simultaneous existence of a marked cyanosis at the extremities and trunk, and of a large and strong pulse like that of a person attacked with a rheumatism? This coincidence shows how difficult and hazardous it is to explain the symptoms of cholera by each other.

In a pathological point of view this case is no less remarkable; the fever during the cyanosis, which existed almost from the commencement of the disease is a very strange anomaly. I have classed this case among the ataxic cases of cholera, on account of the remarkable irregularity and violence of the symptoms. Is this arrangement correct? This case is certainly one of the lightest cases of ataxic cholera that I have ever treated. The remedies in this case acted with a precision and an energy that are scarcely ever witnessed in the common cases of ataxic cholera. After the cyanosis and the distressing cramps had ceased, the chief difficulty was the derangement of the digestive organs. The cramps yielded to Camphor. Carbo-veg. hastened the disappearance of the cyanotic symptoms. Nux-vomica put a stop to the vomiting which continued during the fever.

CASE VI.—*By Dr. Guyton.—Epidemic Cholera ; simple or genuine Cholera.—Cure.*

Gillet, 48 years old, carrier, was a patient in the ward St. Benjamin, No. 4, when he was attacked with cholera the 13th of April. The patient had had the asthma for ten years past, and exhibited all the signs of an advanced pulmonary emphysema. The attacks came on several times in the course of a year ; he had had two this winter. A fortnight previous to his coming to the hospital the patient took a vapor-bath for some cutaneous disease of which no trace remains visible ; he took cold after the bath ; cough, dyspnœa and fever sat in. On coming to the hospital he had an acute inflammatory catarrh on both sides of the chest.

April 13th. Marked improvement ; the paroxysms of nightly dyspnœa were less frequent, the patient expectorated a well assimilated mucous sputa, when the patient was suddenly attacked with a violent diarrhœa, which had already run on for two days before the patient mentioned it ; he had kept it concealed lest his usual allowance should be curtailed. The discharges were quite frequent and consisted of a clear liquid that flowed like water, without effort or colic. Having taken Ipecac. for some days past for his catarrh, it was supposed that it might perhaps be the cause of his diarrhœa ; this drug was discontinued, and a solution of two drops of the spirits of Camphor in a tumblerful of water was ordered.

This evening the patient feels worse, he complains of pain in the stomach, desire to vomit ; cramps. Has three stools of a greyish substance, having a sickly smell, liquid, with a quantity of fibrinous flocks floating through it. As yet no vomiting. No secretion of urine since morning ; bladder empty. At the same time the breathing, which is generally quiet in the day-time, becomes embarassed, the voice is altered, feebler, unequal, hoarse.

The skin is colder than in a normal state, the extremities, especially the lower ones, are cold, likewise the neck, face and the upper portion of the chest likewise. Pulse frequent, small, compressible. Hands and fingers are blueish.

The abdomen is flattened; the epigastric and umbilical regions are painful, whether touched or no. Tongue white-coated, somewhat dry, cold; thirst intense.

Since the morning-visit the patient's features have altered a good deal; the eyes are sunken, the orbits surrounded with a blueish circle, the lips are rather livid. The features are drawn up, expressive of suffering. Mind perfectly clear, is uneasy concerning his condition.

Carbo-veg. 6, in solution, every half hour, and Phosphorus 6, also in solution, every hour, warm cloths. Water sweetened with sugar.

April 14th.—The warmth of the skin is more uniform and somewhat raised. The pulse is a little higher, 100 beats. The cyanosis has almost disappeared.

No sleep last night, embarrassed respiration without any acute paroxysm of dyspnœa. Mucous expectoration. less abundant than usual, a few turns of cough at short intervals; the characteristic symptoms of the former malady are less marked. Voice continues feeble and hoarse.

Since the Phosphorus was given there has been less diarrhœa, only three evacuations in the night, whereas before this, the evacuations took place without any interruption. The last evacuation was still of a grey color, mixed with fibrinous flocks, but more consistent and more homogeneous. Pains at the epigastrium and round the navel; had an attack of a clear substance, mixed with mucous flócks; frequent nausea.

Physiognomy the same as yesterday. Tongue coated white, moist, colder than naturally. Painful cramps at night.

Intense thirst, no secretion of urine.

Veratrum 3, and Carbo-veget. 6, in solution, alternately.

Evening.—Marked improvement. No stool or vomiting this afternoon; nausea and pain in the epigastrium less. The abdomen continues very flat.

Warmth more regular. Pulse frequent, 100. No cramps in the day-time. Same treatment.

April 15th.—Marked improvement. The patient had several good naps. The features look more natural, and the eyes are less sunken. Natural warmth over the whole body, pulse frequent, but more undulating. Cough more frequent, moister, the patient spits up round clots of mucus. The breathing is easier, and the voice has a clearer sound.

The tongue is covered with a sooty, yellowish, thick mucus. No vomiting, but occasional nausea. Unpleasant sensation in the abdomen and stomach, not exactly painful. In the night, three thick papescent stools, coherent, of a deep yellow color.

One discharge of urine in the day-time.

Veratrum 3, in solution, at long intervals.

April 16th.—Heat and circulation normal. The features are almost natural. No pain or nausea; less thirst. Tongue warm, less coating.

Calm night, with refreshing sleep. Two dark-yellow papescent stools, like fæcal diarrhœa. Urinary secretion restored.

Same treatment. Wine and water.

April 17th.—Complete convalescence, features perfectly natural, warmth and circulation likewise.

Stool in form this morning.

There remains a rest of catarrh; the mucous rattling and wheezing is less, the expectoration looks good, dyspnœa gone. The patient rises from bed.

Wine and water, broth.

Discharged cured on the 1st of May.

This case is an example of light cholera of the simple kind. The asthma was not, as we we first feared, a serious complication. We gave Phosphorus in consequence of the continuance of the diarrhœa which seems to have promptly yielded to this drug. Veratrum terminated the treatment. The charcoal which was administered together with the Phosphorus, was given for the purpose of supporting the strength of the patient.

CASE VII.—*Epidemic Cholera of the simple kind. —Cure.—Reported by Dr. Guyton.*

Ward Sainte Anne, No. 6 (female department.)

Uérard, seamtress, 29 years, entered the hospital on the 14th of April.

Good constitution, looked strong; had enjoyed good health previously.

The patient arrived in Paris from the country on the evening of the 8th of April. Next morning was seized with frequent attacks of painless diarrhœa. Last evening was taken with vomiting during the stool. The discharges upwards and downwards were very frequent all night.

April 14th.—On entering the hospital the patient showed the following symptoms. Altered features, deeply-sunken eyes, with livid circle all around; face elongated.

Breathing more frequent than in health; voice altered and feeble; pulse small, disappearing under the least pressure, frequent, 105. Cyanosis of the fingers and hands; blueish lips, and livid color of the face. Marked coldness all over, especially on the extremities, in the face, on the neck, on the upper portions of the thorax; dry skin.

Tongue white coated, moist; intense thirst. Abdomen flat, drawn in; pain in the epigastrium; nausea, almost constant efforts to vomit. During the two or three hours after her arrival at the hospital, she had three attacks of vomiting of a clear watery substance; four grey-colored stools, very liquid, interspersed with clots.

Mind perfectly sound; good amount of strength; a few painful cramps.

Prognosis unfavorable.

Water sweetened with sugar; Veratrum 3, in solution; warm cloths.

In the evening, the warmth of the body is restored; it is quite perceptible almost all over the body; the tongue continues cold. Pulse larger, 120. Restlessness, the patient changes her position all the time, and is not comfortable in any.

Intense thirst. Pains in the whole abdomen; nausea, repeated desire to vomit; pains, sensation of extreme malaise in the region of the stomach.—Two attacks of vomiting in the afternoon; a clear liquid containing a few clots. Three grey-colored stools, resembling a decoction of crushed rice; discharges two dead lumbrici. Stoppage of the urinary secretion.

Painful cramps in the calves. Continued lividity of the hands, neck, face. Frontal headache.

Carbo-veg. 6 every hour. *Arsenicum* 6 every hour, and, in the middle of the night, every two hours.

11 o'clock at night.—No more vomiting, the nausea continues; same restlessness, marked emaciation.

April 15.—Less restless this morning, improved expression of countenance; cessation of the cyanosis. General heat without sweat; warm tongue. Pulse larger, 120. The patient had only short naps in the night;

she complains of malaise, of uneasiness in the extremities. Slight abdominal pains, distress at the stomach, frequent desire to vomit; several attacks of vomiting in the morning; five evacuations at night, the last of which looks rather better, and has a greenish tinge; it is accompanied with a slight emission of urine.

Arsenicum 6, in water, every three hours (tablespoonful doses.)

Evening.—Nausea, frequent vomiting in the afternoon; general state of the patient the same.

Nux-vomica 12, in solution, (same as Arsenicum.)

April 16.—Evident improvement; the cholera-physiognomy continues somewhat. Flushed face, no cyanosis.

Natural temperature; pulse less frequent. Nausea, repeated but scanty vomiting. Warm tongue with yellowish-white coating.

Two good-looking stools, more consistent, of a greenish-yellowish color. Two discharges of urine.

The patient is better. Less restless; the sensitiveness at the epigastrium and the malaise continue; stirring about in the bed causes a return of the nausea.

The abdominal organs seem torpid; the cramps have disappeared.

Nux-vomica 12, in solution, at long intervals.

Evening.—The patient had several naps in the daytime. Warm skin, flushed face, frequent pulse; the reaction continues pretty violent.

The nausea is less.

Same treatment.

April 17th.—The face looks again natural; the eyes are less sunken; the livid margin around the eyes has disappeared. The tongue is covered with a mucous coating, its edges are red; red gums with white border, a certain degree of stomacace. This morning the patient vomited a little watery substance, with green matter sinking to the bottom. No stool, torpid bowels, nausea, not very frequent.

No medicine; wine of Bagnolles.

Evening,—After taking wine twice, the patient was attacked with nausea, malaise; some pain at the stomach; she vomits. Aversion to wine; nausea, weakness, headache. Pulse 100; skin warmer; no stool.

Wine discontinued. *Nux-vomica* 12, in solution.

April 18.—Unrefreshing sleep, which is disturbed by fatiguing dreams that cause the patient anxiety and wake him. Same pulse, heat.

Physiognomy almost natural; the eyes are no longer sunken. Breathing full and easy; voice has a good resonnance.

Tongue coated with mucus, with red borders and tip; some sensitiveness at the epigastrium, now and then an attack of vomiting this morning. No stool.

Pulsatilla 12, in solution; a few spoonfuls of broth.

April. 19.—Same condition. Bilious vomiting in the morning, two in the evening, scanty. No stool. The menses have made their appearance; it is at the regular period.

Continue the *Pulsatilla.*

April 20.—Quiet night. Animated countenance; headache. Natural warmth; pulse 90; sensitiveness at the epigastrium, some attacks of nausea. Slight vomiting; no stool. The menses continue, but not very profusely.

Carbo-veget. 6, in solution; a few spoonfuls of broth.

April 21.—Sleeps in the night and in the day-time; warmth like that of the breath; pulse soft and normal. General condition satisfactory. The nausea has disappeared; thirst moderate.

Tongue moist; slightly coated white; no redness; stomatitis gone; the menses continue.

Appetite: broth, a soup at supper.

April 22.—Decided convalescence; no pain at the

epigastrium, no nausea, vomiting or stool; the menses cease in the evening.

Same diet.

April 23.—Broth, soup, a little chicken. A simple injection for the constipation.

April 24.—Two stools yesterday evening, composed of papescent fæcal matter, and containing several dead lumbrici.

Cina 12, in solution.

Last night three mucous stools preceded by colic and producing an intense burning sensation at the anus. Scanty liquid discharge at each evacuation, without blood. The abdomen is not painful to pressure.

The patient slept badly. In the day-time two stools of the same nature. Several attacks of flushes of heat, and sweat in the face. Thirst; warm skin; pulse 84. No appetite.

Mercurius 6, in solution.

April 26.—Two liquid bilious stools; some colic; no pain at the anus during the evacuation; torpid bowels; general condition good.

The patient complains of lassitude and numbness in the extremities.

Diet. Tincture of rhubarb, one drop in a tumblerful of water.

April 27.—Two bilious stools containing two lumbrici. Cina in solution.

April 28.—General condition good. A stool mixed with pretty hard fæcal matter, appetite returned. Broth, soup.

April 29th.—One portion.

May 1.—The convalescence proceeds regularly.

Discharged on the 10th of May.

This case is distinguished by the gastro-intestinal inflammation that succeeded the cold period, or rather continued after the cold stage had ceased. The expulsion of lumbrici is also an interesting circumstance.

* * *

The first introduction of nourishing food into the stomach excited the gastric affection, which was combated with perseverance. Of course the medicines had to be given agreeably to the symptomatic indications. Every drug having been administered singly, its action was of course more precise and more distinctly perceptible, except during the first night, when the Arsenic was alternated with charcoal.

CASE VIII.—*By Dr. Guyton.—Epidemic Cholera, simple form.—Cure.*

Lefèvre, 22 years old, turner. Was brought to the hospital on the 28th of April, ward St. Benjamin, No. 10.

Has had diarrhœa for four days past; yesterday it was very copious. This day, April 28, the vomiting has commenced. During the day, a stool, six attacks of vomiting of a clear liquid with a greenish tinge; afterwards cramps, coldness, stoppage of the urinary secretion.

Eight o'clock in the evening.—First record of symptoms: Cholera-features, eyes sunken, somewhat livid. Breathing easy, voice feeble and broken. Pulse small, but perceptible and frequent. Cyanosis of the fingers and of the backs of the hands; skin wrinkled, without elasticity. Some coldness of the face, extremities; chest and abdomen have preserved their natural warmth. The lips and tongue are cold.

Tongue moist, slightly coated white; intense thirst. Pain in the epigastrium, with or without pressure; occasional cramps at the stomach. No vomiting or stool during the first examination.

No urine since morning.

Mind perfectly clear; muscular strength well preserved. Painful cramps in the hands and feet recurring at short intervals.

Prognosis is favorable. Veratrine 3, in solution. *

Water sweetened with sugar; warm cloths.

April 29.—Sensible reaction; warm skin all over; pulse full, large, frequent, 90. Sensation of internal heat; head somewhat heavy and painful.

Face flushed, eyes sunken. Tongue white, moist, warm; thirst intense. Since last evening has had four attacks of vomiting of a clear liquid, with a greenish tinge. Three grey-colored cholera-stools of a certain degree of consistence, mixed with numerous clots; the last stool contains a little bilious coloring matter. No discharge of urine. The patient continues to complain of cramps in the hands and feet.

For the reaction *Aconite* 12, in solution, every hour; *Veratrine* 3, in solution, every three hours.

April 30.—Considerable improvement; the temperature of the skin is like that of the respiration; pulse soft, regular, 60. Last night the patient had a nap. Countenance better, the natural expression has returned, the eyes are more prominent. The headache has disappeared. Tongue white-coated, moist; thirst moderate; no pain at the stomach. No vomiting or stool since yesterday. Last night emitted urine, which is now secreted again as in health. Last night had slight attacks of pain in the hands and feet; they have ceased. Appetite.

The patient who coughed some time before the attack, again commenced his coughing; there was no expectoration, and auscultation yielded no sounds.

Gum-water and broths.

May 1.—Decided convalescence. No stool.

Broths and soups.

May 3.—Convalescence is progressing all the time. A regular allowance of food.

Discharged on the 6th of May.

---

* In several cases Veratrine, 3d attenuation, was used instead of Veratrum or the common white Hellebore.

This was a very mild case of simple cholera, as seen by the shortness and light character of the reaction. An improvement was obtained almost immediately after using the remedies.

CASE IX.—*By Dr. Guyton.—Epidemic Cholera of the diarrhœic variety.—Cure.*

Ward Sainte Anne, No. 20. Entered on the 19th of April, at midnight.

A woman, 68 years old, thin, weakly, of a worn-out constitution; had been asthmatic for a long time. For four days past the patient had had a profuse diarrhœa, without colic; she passed a watery liquid. Her appetite had been somewhat preserved, and she had continued her work. This morning, after having taken a little coffee with milk, she was attacked with vomiting and felt weaker than usual; she was taken to the hospital.

Immediately after her arrival, she vomited up a liquid with mucus; her face looked thin, with an expression of anxiety; but without any marked lividity; the skin looks dull and has an earthy color.

Respiration embarrassed; the voice is feebler and more broken than usual; pulse perceptible, frequent; nails and fingers slightly blue.

Tongue moist, cold; intense thirst. Abdomen distended and soft; no pain on pressure.

Cold face and extremities. The patient has no cramps. —Warm cloths; water sweetened with sugar. *Phosphori-acidum* 6, in solution.

The prognosis does not seem unfavorable, but the broken-down state of the patient is somewhat against her.

Towards evening the skin warms up; the pulse is more perceptible; no vomiting; some nausea; no stool; no urinary secretion.

April 20.—Pretty good night; the patient had several naps. Warm skin; pulse pretty full, of normal frequency.

Tongue moist, coated white, rather cold; a good deal of thirst. No vomiting or nausea. Had three liquid, greyish stools in the night, interspersed with clots. Another stool this morning of more consistency, containing green bilious matter. No urine; abdomen soft, not painful. The diarrhœa is less; the day before the discharges were quite frequent. No cramps.

Continue the *Phosphoric-acid.*

Evening.—The patient feels better; thirst continues. No vomiting; another stool like the last; no urine.

April 21.—Quiet night. Skin feels cooler this morning. Pulse 80. Tongue dry and coated white; intense thirst. Last night had a stool composed of green bile and ropy mucus, proceeding undoubtedly from the large gut; no urine.

Mercurius 12, in solution.

Towards evening, the tongue became moist. Voice continues feeble; skin cool. No stool or urine.

April 22.—Same general condition. Green papescent stool, having a deep bilious tinge. A discharge of urine. Tongue dry in the morning, moist in the day-time. Regular secretion of urine.

Continue Mercurius.

April 23.—Sleep; general condition good; pulse and temperature natural. The voice has recovered its resonnance; the patient feels stronger. The thirst is much less; no vomiting or stool; no pain; appetite.

Continue Mercurius; weak broth; wine and water.

April 24.—Convalescent; tongue naturally moist; no stool. Appetite. Broths and soup.

April. 25.—Unexpected and strange change; coldness of the whole body, feeble voice and embarrassed respiration; tongue cold and dry; no stool or vomiting.

Carbo-veg. 6, in solution.

April 26.—Marked improvement; good night, no stool, natural temperature and voice. Appetite.

Continue *Carbo*; wine of Bagnolles; broths and soups.

April 27.—Convalescent.

April 28 and 29.—Regular allowance.

May 2.—The patient complains of frequent cramps in the hands and feet; diarrhœa, had three or four stools in twenty-four hours, composed of a thick, greenish-yellow liquid. No vomiting; tongue moist; thirst moderate. Urinary secretion natural. The general condition is not very unfavorable.

Ipecac. in solution; strict diet.

May 3.—Diarrhœa continues; less cramps, general condition good.

Phosphori-acidum 6, in solution; broths.

May 5.—Cramps.—*Camphor* in solution.

May 6 and 7.—Formication in the hands.—*Arnica* in solution.

May 8.—Convalescent, and continues so to the end; discharged May 26.

This case shows that cholerine has a marked character different from genuine cholera. Although less serious, yet the liability to relapses which characterises this form of cholera, and the frequent recurrence of certain symptoms during the remission, require particular watching.

CASE X.—By Drs. Guyton and M . . . .—*Epidemic Cholera; galopping or black variety.—Death.*

Regreney, 56 years old, cartman, ward St. Benjamin, No. 29. The patient was struck in the sick-room.

April 29.—The patient had been in the hospital for some time to be cured of wandering pains in the extremities, and of headache which was supposed to be of syphilitic origin. Except these symptoms, which, in themselves, did not seem very important, the patient who was a tall, stout and strong man, enjoyed good health. For two days past he had had diarrhœa; he said nothing of it lest he should have to diet; he even ate some of the food that other patients left on their plates. This morning, after having taken bread and milk for breakfast, he went in the yard at 6 o'clock; in a few moments he felt sick, and asked one of the male nurses to help him up-stairs again.

An hour after we discovered the following symptoms; Features altered, eyes sunken; dark and livid color round the eyes, on the cheeks, at the ears, round the mouth, especially the chin. Lips violet colored; tongue moist and cold, quite blue; expression of anxiety.

Breathing superficial, embarrassed, hurried, with dilatation of the nasal wings; voice feeble and broken.

Pulse collapsed, a slight tremor is perceived from time to time. Marked cyanosis; the skin, neck, thorax and upper extremities are quite livid, the hands and forearms are blue. On the lower limbs a thick veinous network is perceived; the larger veins are engorged. Skin without elasticity; cold all over; profuse, clammy, cold sweat.

Pain in the epigastrium on pressure, acute, intensely painful and frequent cramps. Vomits a liquid resembling water. Rice-water discharges from the bowels, with a few clots. Abdomen rather distended.

Mind perfectly clear, but great anxiety concerning his condition; restlessness. Painful cramps in the hands, calves, stomach. They never cease, and cause the patient to moan.

Dr. Tessier saw him at 9 o'clock. During the examination all the symptoms grew perceptibly worse. Thinking that it was of the highest importance to restore the circulation, Tessier applied Mayor's hammer four times to the præcordial region. The pain was acutely felt, but the pulse did not return.

Prognosis extremely unfavorable; the patient sank lower and lower.

Arsenicum 6, in solution.—Warm cloths.

Two o'clock.—Pulse perceptible, pretty full even, but the cyanosis is worse; the whole body looks livid. Clammy sweat, skin somewhat warm. The hammer has caused neither blister nor redness of the epidermis. The breathing becomes more and more embarrassed, the tracheal rattle is heard at a distance.

Vomiting, two scanty stools of clear water.

Alcoholic solution of *Chamomile.*

Nine o'clock.—The whole body looks livid and has a blueish tinge, as if ecchymosed. Loss of consciousness and speech, death-rattle. Died at two o'clock in the morning.

Post-mortem examination thirty hours after death. —The external aspect of the corpse is that of a strong man; broad shoulders, good muscular development of the extremities, a certain stoutness.

The whole surface of the body has a blueish tinge. Here and there large livid spots.—Excessive rapidity of the extremities.

Abdomen.—Vascular engorgement of the coats of the bowels. This vascular injection, although deep-seated, imparts a red tinge to the whole surface of the circonvolutions.—No serum in the peritoneal cavity.

The intestinal canal having been opened, it was washed in a quantity of water; the mucous membrane, from the stomach to the rectum, presented a general inflammation, of which we shall endeavor to furnish a detailed and correct description.

Stomach: Injected state of all the vessels; clusters of congested vessels composed of straight lines without any curves; vessels along whose borders the blood had oozed out; the whole mucous membrane had a reddish tinge; numerous ecchymoses of various sizes, from that of a point to that of a five-cent piece; these ecchymosed spots are of a tolerably bright-red color. No ulcerations.

The inflammation is more distinct at the larger ex

tremity of the stomach, and along the small curvature than in the pyloric region.

Duodenum.—Same alterations as in the stomach. The inflammation was very distinct on the intestinal surface of the symptoms, and more acute in the first than in the second half of the duodenum.

Small intestine.—The inflammation extends through the whole length of the small intestine: general congestion of the vessels, diffuse redness, numerous ecchymoses. The valvulæ conniventes are very prominent. Here and there a portion of the mucous membrane looks healthy; but the same alterations which we have just described, reappear a little further on.

Towards the middle of the jejunum a number of small granulations are seen, which raise the mucous membrane and form a sort of miliary eruption. These scarcely-perceptible granulations contrast with the remaining mucous membrane by their pale-white color. They seem to consist of scattered follicles. As they progress towards the extremity of the small intestine, they become less numerous, but bigger and more prominent. Several seem united and agglomerated, and form irregular elevations, whereas, in the other parts, they are regularly rounded. Peyer's glands are prominent, and the more the nearer they are to the ileo-cœcal valve. They show no signs of vascular injection; no red points, ecchymoses, or ulceration are perceived in any of them. Their surface looks white and pale like that of isolated follicles.

It should be observed that the inflammation is less marked towards the end of the lesser intestine than towards the duodenum; the same phenomenon presented itself in the stomach where the inflammation was more intense in the cardiac than in the pyloric region.

The upper surface of the ileo-cœcal valve is covered with a large number of big isolated follicles of a regular round shape, white color like that of the mucous membrane, on which they constitute little prominences and which, in this place, is neither red nor congested.

Large intestine.—The lower surface of the ileo-cœcal valve exhibits symptoms of intense inflammation) striking analogy to the pyloric valve); this inflammation extends throughout the cœcum and the large intestine, but seems much more marked in the cœcum than in the colon or in the sygmoid flexure.

No ulceration.

We omitted to mention that the intestinal canal did not contain a trace of fæcal matter. It was full of a clear, almost inodorous liquid, in which floated small flocks of a whitish-grey color that imparted to it the appearance of rice-water or soup-suds.

Compared to the remarkable alterations in the intestinal mucous membrane, the other organs were but triflingly affected.

The vena cava and all the abdominal veins were filled with a black, thick, viscous blood.

The liver had a brown color; all the hepatic vessels, especially the ramifications of the vena porta, were filled with a black blood.

The spleen was flabby and pale. The kidneys did not show any marked change. The bladder was contracted, empty and shrunk.

The right ventricle of the heart was distended with a large quantity of very dark blood; the left ventricle was almost empty, but not much contracted.

The lungs were perfectly sound.

The brain was not examined.

This case of black cholera is exceedingly characteristic. In 1832 I had often succeeded in rousing the vital forces by applying Mayor's hammer, dipped in boiling water, to the epigastrium and the region of the heart; in the present case the application had no effect, although it caused pain.

As regards the gastro-intestinal inflammation revealed by the post-mortem examination, we shall recur to it again in our therapeutic analysis of these cases.

CASE XI. *By Dr. Guyton.—Ataxic Cholera.—Death.*

Riquet, 39 years, entered the hospital on the first of May, 1848, at two o'clock in the afternoon, ward St. Benjamin, No. 3.

Had enjoyed good health previously, had led a regular life. While doing his errands in Paris, the day previous, the patient had been taken with diarrhœa; in the evening he complained of weariness, malaise, did not want any supper. During the night discharges increased in frequency, and about nine o'clock, this morning, vomiting set in; the patient grew cold, was seized with cramps in the extremities; the urinary secretion had stopped.

On entering the hospital, we found his features altered, expressive of uneasiness and distress; eyes sunken, face elongated.

Breathing embarrassed, anxious; voice feeble, broken; coldness of the extremities, face, neck, upper portions of the chest; cold and clammy sweat; pulse almost imperceptible; from time to time a few feeble pulsations are perceived. On auscultating the heart, only a distant tremor is perceived. Cyanosis of the hands, forearms; blueish tint of the arms, marked lividity of the lips, tongue, interior of the eyes and mouth. Cyanosis of the lower extremities, a dense network of veins.

Tongue moist, cold, covered with a compact yellowish-white coating. The abdomen is somewhat distended; acute pain in the epigastrium, even without pressure. The vomiting is quite frequent, and the nausea continues uninterruptedly; the alvine evacuations set in at short intervals; they are composed of a clear, grey liquid mixed with a few clots and are passed almost involuntarily. Complete suppression of urine. Bladder empty.

Mind perfectly clear; the patient is uneasy, anxious; one of his relatives had died of cholera, he thinks he cannot recover.

Painful cramps in the hands, legs and stomach.

The general appearance of the patient, and an analysis of the symptoms, lead to an extremely unfavorable diagnosis. The patient is drowsy; the eyelids are only half closed, the eyes are without any expression; the head feels heavy, painful; prostration of strength.

Veratrine 3, in solution, a tablespoonful every 15 minutes, alternated with *Carbo-veg.* every half hour.

Mayor's hammer is applied four times; the pain is felt, but the pulse remains unchanged.

Five o'clock in the evening.—Vomiting, two discharges from the bowels, consisting of a clear liquid with clots. Some coldness of the skin; pulse very feeble, but regular and perceptible; breathing superficial and anxious; drowsiness, pain and heaviness of the head; cramps.

Eleven o'clock.—General condition of the patient worse, drowsiness more marked, physiognomy unfavorable. The patient answers only when urged, then falls asleep again; the breathing is embarrassed, the pulse becomes collapsed; coldness; increased cyanosis of the face, hands, cold sweats.

Arsenicum in solution, every 15 minutes, alternated with *Carbo-veg.* in solution every half hour.

May 2.—The general appearance of the patient is somewhat improved; the eyes have more expression, the face is a little more animated. Breathing freer; the skin of the face, neck and extremities is cold; pulse feeble but regular; head not so heavy.

Little vomiting; four rice-water discharges, the two

last of which have a slightly yellowish tint; abdomen flat, not painful to pressure. Thirst intense. No urine.

Cramps not frequent.

Arsenicum 6, in solution, every hour.

The hammer raised a blister, which soon collapsed again; there was scarcely a little redness round the spot where the instrument had been applied; it soon disappeared again. Scarcely any reaction.

Evening.—Skin cold, pulse very small; cold clammy sweat in the face and on the neck. The cramps have disappeared. The headache continues; no vomiting or pain in the epigastrium. Three liquid stools mixed with yellowish clots; no urine.

Breathing embarrassed, sighing.

Arsenicum 6, in solution, every hour.

May 3.—Headache, countenance without expression, drowsiness, eyes half closed. The patient answers questions as if yielding to entreaties, and then sinks back again into a state of apathy. Tongue moist and cold, slightly coated white; thirst moderate. Voice feeble, breathing embarrassed, sighing. The pulse is small, frequent; skin cold, covered with clammy sweat in the face, on the neck, upper extremities; the lividity is less.

Thirst. No vomiting. Last night had several liquid stools resembling in color a solution of ratañia and depositing a few clots of fæcal matter. This color probably arose from the pressure of a little blood. No urine.

Nux-vomica 6, in solution.—*Carbo-veg*. 6, in solution.

Evening.—Same skin and pulse. Breathing more embarrassed; at every moment the patient utters deep sighs. Drowsiness and restlessness; patient turns about in his bed, uncovers himself, keeps changing the position of his limbs all the time.

In the afternoon, good-looking evacuation mixed with fæcal matter.

Midnight.—Increased coldness in the face, on the chest and arms; the clammy sweat is colder. Increased drowsiness, it is difficult to get an answer from the patient. Pulse very small.

Arsenicum and *Carbo-veg.* in solution, every 15 minutes alternately.

May 4.—Same as last evening. Two stools of bilious fæcal matter of ordinary quantity and having a good appearance. No vomiting, no discharge of urine. Abdomen flat and drawn in.

The drowsiness continues; frequent sighing breathing; physiognomy without expression; cyanosis ceases.

Opium 12, in solution.

Five o'clock in the evening.—Same drowsiness, same coldness; pulse filiform.

Distilled water of laurocerasus, two teaspoonsful.

Nine o'clock—More laurocerasus water had been given than had been ordered. The patient continued to sink; the breathing became more embarrassed; tracheal rattle set in; complete prostration and loss of expression in the countenance, collapse of pulse. Towards the end the temperature of the body rose again; the chest and arms were covered with a warm moisture, but the face remained cold, covered with a clammy sweat.

At 10 o'clock the patient died.

This case shows that the vomiting and cramps had been stopped, the alvine evacuations had been considerably modified in their quality; but it was impossible to restore the urinary secretion or to bring on a reaction on the skin or in the circulation.

Post-mortem examination.—On opening the abdominal cavity, the peritoneal surface of the bowels was found red, injected; the circumvolutions are marked with small, narrow streaks, arising from fine clusters of more intensely-congested vessels of the peritoneum at these points. The peritoneal cavity does not contain any liquid or other abnormal secretions.

The small intestine was found to contain a yellow, thick, coherent substance.

The stomach contained some of the beverage. The internal surface of the stomach showed unmistakeable signs of inflammation: redness, turgescence without softening of the mucous membrane; dotted with fine clusters of congested capillaries; numerous ecchymosed spots of an intense redness within the thickness of the coats; the mucous coat shows such lesions throughout its whole extent.

Same condition of the duodenum; in the ileum similar congestions and ecchymoses were seen; no peculiar alteration of the glands of Peyer; a few inches above the ileo-cœcal valve and near the opening of the ileum into the cœcum a dense, grey-colored rash of the size of a pin's head is perceived. In the cœcum and at the commencement of the large intestine, the mucous membrane exhibited clusters of congested capillaries, with a few intensely-red places, here and there, and red ecchymosed spots more scantily disseminated, all pointing to an intense gastro-enteritis. The mesenteric ganglia looked swollen and red.

No alteration of the spleen or liver. No urine in the bladder.

The abdominal veins, and the trunk of the vena cava were filled with a black, fluid blood, without coagula, and containing scarcely a few thickened clots.

Brain.—A little clear serum in the meningeal membranes. At the union of the lower third of the lateral surfaces of the brain with the two upper thirds, there was on each side a well-marked, red semicircular streak going from behind forward. This streak arose from the injected condition of the meningeal membranes in that region, and from a densely-dotted redness of the cerebral substance penetrating to a certain depth. Round these dots the meningeal membranes and the cerebral substance are slightly adhering.

Lower surface: the cineritious substance is evidently congested; the pia-mater in this region is redder than the neighboring parts. Continuing the cerebral fissure by an incision, the middle ventricle was opened, and the annular protuberance and the rachidian bulb were divided in the middle. These parts exhibited a well-marked persistent yellowish-white color, diminishing as it extended towards the rachidian bulb, where it disappeared altogether. The surrounding parts exhibited no abnormal changes either in regard to consistence or color. There was a little light-colored serum in the ventricles.

No other changes of consequence were noticed.

This case of ataxic cholera is remarkable on account of the course which the disease ran, of the progressive aggravation of the cerebral affection, the first symptoms of which were seen from the very commencement of the malady. The cessation of the actual cholera-symptoms was not accompanied with a true reaction, and the patient finally succombed in a state of coma, coldness and cyanosis.

The inflammatory symptoms revealed by the post-mortem examination, deserve the attention of observers. We have seen that they existed in the black variety of cholera, consequently during the cold stage; in this case we find them to exist after the disease had run for some days.

CASE XII.—*By Dr. Guyton.—Simple Cholera.—Cure.*

Miller, 35 years old, mason, entered on the 3d of May, in the Ward St. Benjamin, No. 6.

On the 19th of April, the patient was taken with malaise and diarrhœa; nevertheless he continued his work. On the 2d of May he stayed home, being weaker;

he had a great many passages. On the 3d, at noon, the diarrhœa was still worse; what he passed was said to resemble flour-water; afterwards vomiting set in; soon after coldness and cramps.

At eight o'clock in the evening, the following symptoms had developed themselves: emaciation, prominence of the cheek-bones, sunken eyes; marked lividity around the eyes, mouth, chin. Frontal headache.

Voice feeble, broken; the breathing did not seem embarassed. Cyanosis of the hands. Pulse perceptible, regular, frequent, small. Coldness all over, especially in the face, at the neck, on the upper extremities; these parts are covered with a cold, clammy sweat; coldness of the lower limbs.

Tongue moist, icy-cold; intense thirst. Abdomen flat, drawn-in, sensible to pressure. After entering the hospital, he was taken with copious vomiting which the patient had taken to get a little warm. During the day he had twenty-two stools. A few drops of urine were passed.

Understanding perfectly clear; his strength was not much less; cramps easier.

Veratrine 3, in solution, every half hour. Water and sugar.

May 4.—No sleep; restless. The skin is warmer; pulse pretty full and frequent. Tongue coated white, moist, still cold; abdomen drawn in. Thirst intense, with nausea; two copious vomitings mixed with little clots. Watery stool, precipitating a green deposit resembling chopped greens. No urine. Frequent cramps in the calves and hands.

Continue the Veratrine every two hours.

In the evening the heat of the skin was less uniform; the face, forearms, upper part of the chest, were covered with a cold clammy sweat. The pulse was small and frequent. Intense thirst; the patient had used several times the chair standing by the side of his bed.

Face and hands livid; restlessness, headache; the patient turns about all the time, uncovers himself. Cramps.

Arsenicum 6, every half hour; afterwards every hour,

May 5.—General condition better, some sleep. Temperature more regular, improved in quality; pulse full and frequent. The skin is less livid, assumes its ordinary appearance. Tongue white, moist, cool; thirst less intense. Two stools: the first grey and thick, the second of a slightly-yellowish appearance. Scanty emission of urine this morning. The cramps have ceased entirely.

Arsenicum in solution every two hours.

In the evening, powerful reaction; striking rise of temperature, congested condition of the face, eyes; pulse full, large, frequent. Tongue warm; rather dry; thirst moderate. Headache. Every trace of the cyanosis has disappeared. Neither vomiting nor alvine discharges; discharge of urine.

Aconite 3, in solution, every hour.

May 6.—Skin cooler, of a good temperature: pulse regular, soft, of middling frequency. The patient had several naps. Uneasiness rather than pain in the bowels; no vomiting. A stool of a dark-yellow color. The urinary secretion is completely restored.—Physiognomy natural; the sound of the voice likewise.

Continue the Aconite.

No stool during the day.

May 7.—General condition good; temperature of the skin like the warmth of the breath. Pulse normal. The headache has ceased. No thirst, vomiting or stool. Appetite.

Carbo-veg. in solution.

May 8.—Diarrhœic stool; no pain in the bowels; the patient wants to eat.

Continue the *Carbo-vegetabilis*; a few spoonfuls of broth; wine and water.

May 9.—Convalescent; neither vomiting nor alvine evacuations. Appetite.—Broths, soups.

The convalescence goes regularly. The patient was discharged cured on the 19th of May.

This was a very simple case. The symptoms which did not yield to Veratrine, at once yielded to Arsenic; Aconite promptly arrested the excessive reaction. *Carbo-veget.* was given for the purpose of supporting the patient's strength.

CASE XIII.—*By Dr. Guyton.—Simple Cholera.—Cure.*

Sainty, 28 years old, carrier, admitted May 4th, ward St. Benjamin, No. 9.

This patient was habitually intemperate; had been drinking all this week; for the last two days had had diarrhœa, in spite of which he continued his work and mode of life. This day, May 4th, at noon, the alvine discharges set in uninterruptedly, accompanied by vomiting and cramps.

Three o'clock.—Cholera features; eyes sunken, surrounded with a blueish circle; lips and and tongue livid.

Breathing rather short and accelerated; voice very feeble. Pulse imperceptible. Cyonosis of the fingers; veins swollen, no circulation on the dorsal surface of the hands; the remainder of the skin had its natural color, but had lost its elasticity. Marked coldness, especially of the extremities, face, neck, upper portion of the chest, these parts are covered with a cold and clammy sweat.

Tongue blueish, cold, moist, coated white; intense thirst. Abdomen drawn in; pain on pressure in the epigastric and umbilical regions; cramps in the stomach. Renewed vomiting; after entering the ward he vomited up a white-colored liquid, which was followed by a clear watery stool, mixed with a few clots. No urine.

Understanding clear, good amount of strength. Frequent and painful cramps in the calves, feet, hands and stomach.

Prognosis unfavorable; great disturbance of the vital and natural functions; at the end of a few hours, intense coldness, arrest of the circulation.

Veratrine 3, in solution, every 15 minutes; water and sugar; warm flannels.

In the evening the patient had not warmed up; no return of the pulse. Cold, clammy sweat. Voice feeble; breathing short and hurried. Frontal headache; buzzing in the ears, drowsiness. The patient does every thing in his bed without knowing it. Vomiting ceases; intense thirst. Painful cramps succeeding each other at short intervals.

Arsenicum 6, in solution.

Midnight.—The cramps continue without intermission, they cause the patient to moan and make him very restless.

Camphor in solution.

May 5.—Improvement; the cramps are not frequent; the temperature has risen, is cool and uniform; pulse small, regular, not frequent. No vomiting; two stools; a discharge of urine.

Arsenicum in solution, every two hours.

In the evening, violent headache, of which the patient complains a good deal. The skin has a good temperature; the pulse becomes fuller. The cyanosis disappears. Intense thirst; pain in the epigastrium; four vomitings one after the other, composed of a white, watery liquid. No stool; emission of urine.

Cessation of the cramps since four o'clock in the afternoon.

Nux-vomica 3, in solution, every hour.

Midnight.—Two attacks of vomiting, with a slightly greenish tinge.

May 6.—Same condition of the skin and pulse; no cyanosis. Headache, fatiguing buzzing in the ears. Tongue moist, coated white; intense thirst; pain in the epigastrium, green vomiting; no stool.

The patient had a little nap; return of the cramps.

Pulsatilla in solution.

In the evening, two cholera-stools, with little clots, a slight bilious tinge. Vomiting. Headache.

Belladonna 3, in solution.

May 7.—Gentle warmth of the skin, without sweat, good pulse. The physiognomy is improved; the eyes are less sunken. Pain in the epigastrium; three vomitings, the two last of which were mixed with bilious matter. Yellowish stool.

Less headache; return of strength. The breathing easy, and the voice has resumed its natural sound.

In the evening, intense thirst, sensitiveness of the epigastrium. Neither vomiting nor stool. Heaviness of the head, drowsiness.

Opium 3 in solution.

May 8.—Green vomiting; three bilious stools. Less headache.

Ipecacuanha in solution.

During the day, the patient vomited once and had a stool.

Aconite in solution.

May 9.—Vomited once; three good-looking stools, with fæcal matter. Appetite.

Pulsatilla in solution.—Broths.

May 10.—No headache; no pain in the epigastrium; less thirst. Appetite. General condition good.

Continue *Pulsatilla*. Broths.

May 11.—No vomiting, a stool in form; appetite; convalescence.—Broths; soups.

May 13.—Continued convalescence. The last two days the patient had three meals. Discharged cured.

In the previous cases I have purposely directed attention to the symptoms of gastro-enteritis revealed by the post-mortem examination. This inflammatory condition has to be struggled against in simple cholera after the actual cholera-symptoms have ceased, as was the case in the case before us.

CASE XIV.—*By Dr. Guyton.—Simple Cholera.—Cure.*

Tirfoin (a consumptive patient, who was attacked in the ward while under treatment for phthisis), 52 years old, doing errands, admitted April 21st, ward St. Benjamin, No. 16. Was in the last stage of consumption, emaciated and very feeble.

Last evening, May 4th, he complained for the first time of a diarrhœa that had set in the night previous; frequent liquid stools without colic; the patient was up a good part of the day, had only taken some broth. At the evening-visit, was ordered to take *Acidum-phosphoricum*, 6.

May 5.—Altered features, lividity of the face, sunken eyes. Frequent and embarrassed breathing, aphonia.

Pulse perceptible, very small, frequent; cyanosis of the face, hands and legs. Coldness all over, especially in the face, at the neck and hands; clammy sweat.

Tongue blueish, cold, moist, coated white; intense thirst, sensation of internal heat. Pain in the epigastric and umbilical regions; abdomen hollow, drawn in. No vomiting. A great many watery colorless discharges from the bowels. A scanty discharge of urine towards morning.

Prostration, weakness; no cramps.

Ipecacuanha 3, in solution; water and sugar; warm flannels.

Evening.—During the day the temperature of the

skin had continued to sink; the pulse is still weaker, frequent. Intense thirst; no vomiting, nausea. Frequent stools, which the patient discharges involuntarily; they are absorbed by the cloths, but leave no stain. No urine.

The patient lies on his back, is prostrated, no cramps.

Arsenicum 6 and *Carbo-veget.* 6, in alternation, every half hour.

Midnight.—General condition the same.—Vomits up a clear liquid with flocks. Scanty emission of urine.

Now and then a little cough; during the day had not raised the fourth part of the purulent matter which he had raised previously.

May 6.—No sleep. The general condition is rather better, the skin warmer, covered with a tepid sweat; the pulse is stronger, the lividity less. Tongue cold, rather dry; intense thirst. Abdomen drawn in, painful in the epigastric region, no vomiting; three copious stools resembling a decoction of ground rice. Discharge of urine.

Arsenicum and *Carbo-veget.* continued at long intervals.

Evening.—The temperature of the skin is improved; no sweat; pulse rather full and regular. No vomiting; three involuntary discharges from the bowels which scarcely stain the linen.

May 7.—Perceptible improvement; the face has lost its livid color, looks natural; the voice is firmer and stronger. The patient coughs more, raises more. The temperature of the skin is mild, uniform, like that of the breath; no sweat; good pulse. Tongue moister, less thirst. Some pain in the epigastrium; this morning the patient had a stool of more consistence and yellow. Two discharges of urine in the night.

Ipecacuanha and *Carbo-veget.* 6, in solution, alternately.

Evening.—The patient is better; stronger; he helps

himself, turns about in his bed. No stool, discharge of urine; raises profusely, a thick matter.

May 8.—Good temperature of the skin; pulse normal. No vomiting, some diarrhœa. The phthisicky symptoms re-appear.

Carbo-veget. in solution. Broths, water and wine.

Evening.—No stool. Frequent cough, and profuse expectoration. The former condition has set in again. He died a month after of his disease.

This case shows the efficacy of Arsenic and Carbo-veg. administered alternately. The temporary suspension of the symptoms of phthisis during the violence of the cholera is a phenomenon common to phthisis as well as to other forms of disease.

CASE XV.—*By Dr. Guyton.—Ataxic Cholera.—Death.*

Duhamel, 35 years old, fruit-merchant, admitted May 7th, in the ward Sainte-Anne, No. 16.

This woman who had enjoyed good health previously, was taken with diarrhœa in the afternoon; the discharges were frequent; but she had no pain, and continued her work as usual, and ate prawns at supper. During the night the diarrhœa continued; about twenty stools in 24 hours. At 10 o'clock this morning the vomitings set in, which were soon after followed by cramps and coldness.

Record of symptoms at one o'clock in the afternoon: Cholera-physiognomy, sunken eyes, elongated features, lividity of the face and blueness of the lips.

Breathing easy, aphonia. Pulse very small, of normal frequency. Intense cyanosis of the hand, lividity of the forearms; the veins are swollen, blueish, cyanosis of the feet, lividity of the legs and thighs. Marked coldness of the whole body, especially of the neck, face, upper part of the chest, arms; cold and clammy sweat.

Tongue moist, coated white. Thirst moderate. Painfulness to pressure in the epigastrium; abdomen not drawn in. Seven attacks of vomiting, one of which took place immediately after admission in the hospital; a quantity of liquid clear as water, coming up by mouthfuls without any effort. Frequent stools, resembling rice-water with a few little clots. Constant nausea. No urine.

Mind perfectly clear. Headache, buzzing in the ears; sensation of internal heat. Painful cramps in the feet, calves and hands, recurring at short intervals.

Veratrine 3, in solution, every half hour. Water and sugar, warm cloths.

Evening.—Return of warmth on the chest, abdomen and arms; these parts are covered with a warm moisture. The face and neck continue cold and are covered with a clammy sweat. Tongue coated white, almost dry; thirst. No vomiting, three liquid stools passed in the bed; no urine.

Headache, restlessness; the patient changes her position all the time, moans a good deal, is uneasy. Breathing embarrassed, hurried. Painful cramps.

Arsenicum 6, in solution, every half hour.

May 8.—Extremely restless all night; the temperature of the skin has sunk; cold moisture in the face, on the neck, chest, arms. Pulse very small, filiform. Tongue cold, dry; thirst moderate. Acute pains at the epigastrium, nausea, no vomiting in the night. Liquid involuntary stools, scarcely staining the linen. No urine.

Breathing embarrassed, short, hurried; intense lividity of the face, neck, forearms, legs. Restless, uneasy, the patient moans constantly. Frequent cramps. Prognosis very doubtful.

Continue *Arsenicum*.

Evening.—Same symptoms; temperature, sweat, pulse, restlessness the same as in the morning. The breathing is more embarassed; pains at the base of the thorax caused by every attempt at drawing breath. Cramps on moving the legs ever so little.

Tongue thick, dry, coated white; thirst moderate. Vomiting, several stools, one on the chamber; a white, clear liquid, with little clots; tenesmus of the bladder which causes much distress; a spoonful of colored urine is drawn off by means of the catheter.

Camphor, in solution, every hour.

May 9.—Pulse imperceptible; dark cyanosis of the face, marked emaciation; violet color of the hands, fore-arms and legs. Short and frequent breathing; acute pains at the base of the thorax; painful tenesmus of the bladder without intermission. No urine is obtained by the catheter. Tongue white and dry. The patient is sinking, scarcely answers any questions. Complete stoppage of all the secretions.

Carbo-veget. 6, every 10 minutes.

During the day the breathing becomes worse, coma sets in; hands and legs are covered with violet-colored spots. The patient dies at 9 o'clock in the evening.

Post-mortem examination.—The stomach contains a large quantity of a grey-colored liquid. The mucous coat of the large curvature presents a clustered and dotted appearance arising from congested capillaries, with a few well-marked ecchymoses; it is turgescent and softened. Similar alterations here and there at the lesser curvature and in the duodenal region.

The small intestine contains a quantity of a grey-colored liquid, with little clots. Here and there the mucous membrane looks red, owing to capillary congestion; no ecchymoses. In the lower third the glands of Peyer are grey and prominent; confluent miliary granulations, especially in the region of the ileo-cœcal valve. No change in the large intestine; the mesenteric ganglia are red and somewhat swollen.

The liver and spleen are sound. Bladder empty.

Lungs sound; the parenchyma not congested, and crepitates throughout. The right ventricle and the venæ cavæ were filled with a black, viscous, congulated blood. Left ventricle empty and contracted.

Brain sound.

In this case, an incomplete remission set in, and soon after all the phenomena got worse, amidst a restlessness and an anguish, which were followed by coma and death, without being in the least degree modified by treatment. We direct attention to the ecchymoses of the cyanosed parts, in order to justify our views concerning the congestive character of the cyanosis.

CASE XVI.—*By Dr. Guyton.—Ataxic Cholera.—Death.*

Michel, 46 years old, blind, admitted May 7th, ward St. Benjamin, No. 10.

Sound constitution; looks strong, is fleshy. This man had worked hard all this time, but had lived moderately. At 7 o'clock in the morning, he was suddenly taken with diarrhœa without any precursory symptoms; in a few hours vomiting set in, and lastly cramps and coldness.

Admitted at 5 o'clock in the evening.—The features look almost natural; some lividity round the eyes which look dull, empty and are sunken; lividity round the lips and chin; lips blue. Frontal headache; buzzing in the ears.

Respiration embarrassed; the patient complains of pain and oppression. When drawing breath; voice perfectly natural. No pulse. Cyanosis of the hands; the whole body is cold, only the chest is a little warm. The skin is covered with a cold and clammy moisture.

Tongue cold, quite blue, coated white; thirst very great. Pain at the epigastrium, with or without contact. The abdomen which is covered with fat, is of a normal size. Vomited six times during the day; once after coming to the hospital, only a little; nausea, constant distress at the epigastrium. Frequent stools having the usual cholera-appearance; no urine.

Mind perfectly clear; the patient walked to the hospital from the neighboring street, supported by two friends. Frequent and painful cramps in the hands and legs. Restlessness; the patient turns in his bed all the time; sensation of burning heat internally.

The attack is violent and sudden; the vital and natural functions are intensely effected. It is feared that no reaction may set in in such a fat person. Warm cloths, water and sugar.

Arsenicum 6 and *Carbo-veget.* 6, both in solution, alternately every half hour.

Midnight.——Excessively restless, constant tossing about. The patient uncovers himself, throws off the warm flannels; he complains of much heat. Constant moaning, embarrassed respiration, as if proceeding from spasmodic suffocation; since this symptom set in, the cramps ceased. Same skin and pulse. No vomiting; three watery stools, with a few clots.

Camphor, in solution, every half hour.

May 8.—Same temperature, with clammy and cold moisture. A few beats of the pulse. Less oppression, but the respiration continues embarrassed.

Tongue dry, with a thick white coating; thirst. Pain in the epigastrium when pressing upon it; the abdomen has the natural size. No vomiting; nausea. Three liquid stools, with clots; the last stool looks yellow. No urine.

Mind perfectly clear; the voice has a natural sound; the features are not much altered, constituting a striking contrast with a deep-seated derangement of the other functions.

The restlessness continues; return of the cramps, not very frequently.

Arsenicum 6, in solution, every half hour.

In the evening, the patient is cold all over, even the chest and abdomen; these parts are covered with a clammy sweat. No pulse. Increased cyanosis of the face and hands. Breathing hurried. Tongue dry, coated white; intense thirst. Pain in the epigastric and umbilical regions when pressing upon these parts. Three attacks of vomiting; five green-colored stools. No urine.

Less restlessness and cramps.

There never was a single sign of genuine reaction; the pulse remained collapsed, the skin cold, without any appreciable change of temperature. The discharges looked better towards the end, but this had no effect upon the disease. In the night the patient became comatose, sank, tracheal rattle set in, and he died at 7 o'clock in the morning.

Post-mortem examination.—Considerable accumulation of fat in the sub-cutaneous cellular tissue, in the mesentery, epiploon, and around the abdominal viscera.

The stomach contained a certain quantity of green-colored liquid. The small intestine was shrunk, of very small volume, containing a thick, yellow pap of good appearance. Clusters of very fine congested capillaries, and dotted appearance; small red ecchymoses scattered here and there over the mucous coat of the stomach; in the congested portions this coat is turgid, but not softened. Same condition of the mucous membrane of the duodenum and the superior portion of the small intestine; a similar appearance of this membrane in the last third of the intestine, where the glands of Peyer are moreover grey and prominent, like a confluent miliary rash.

Red places scattered throughout the large gut.

Abdominal viscera all sound.

Lungs and brain normal.

The right ventricle and the venæ cavæ are filled with

a blood that is scarcely coagulated, and is sticky like pitch. The left ventricle is empty and shrunk.

This case is interesting on account of the irregularity of the symptoms. The face and voice remained almost natural; complete cyanosis, with complete collapse of pulse at the extremities. Restlessness, spasms, dyspnœa; lastly coma, stertorous breathing, preceded by a marked improvement of the evacuations.

CASE XVII.—*By Dr. Guyton.—Diarrhœic Cholera.—Cure.*

Hiolle, 16 years old, admitted May 7th, ward St. Benjamin, No. 32.

On the 6th he was taken with diarrhœa, without colic; next morning, vomiting supervened. Was admitted in the evening of the 6th.

No great change in the features; the countenance looks less animated than in health; the eyes are sunken; there is paleness, but no lividity. Breathing and voice pretty natural. Pulse frequent, compressible. Marked cyanosis of the fingers and back of the hands; skin cool, but not cold.

Tongue moist, coated white; thirst. Abdomen not drawn in, with painfulness of the epigastric and umbilical regions with or without pressure. In the afternoon, frequent stools and vomiting. Voided urine once only in 24 hours. No cramps.

May 8.—Same symptoms. Vomited three times, a clear, watery liquid; four yellowish, liquid stools. Urinated once.

Ipecacuanha, in solution

May 9.—Hotter than in health, the pulse is more frequent; the backs of the hands continue to look livid. Tongue somewhat dry, thirst. Green-colored vomiting, yellow-liquid stools. Urinated once in 24 hours.

Veratrine 3, in solution.

May 10.—Temperature and pulse good; some traces

4*

of cyanosis on the hands. Tongue moist; thirst moderate. Sensitiveness of the epigastrium to pressure; two attacks of vomiting, two bilious stools which are very liquid. Discharge of urine. Appetite.

Broths. *Nux-vomica* 3, in solution.

In the day-time, the patient had eaten some chocolate that had been given to him by his friends. In the evening he complained of distress, looked pale, had chills, pain at the epigastrium, an attack of vomiting, and several copious stools.

Nux-vomica, in solution, as before.

May 11.—Temperature and pulse good. The effects of yesterday's excess have not yet disappeared entirely; this morning had a clear liquid yellow stool, with deposits of little clots. No vomiting; discharge of urine.

Bryonia 3, in solution.

Evening.—Sensitiveness of the epigastrium, three turns of vomiting, with a greenish tinge; two stools, the latter rather thick, yellow, not very copious.

May 12.—Sensitiveness of the epigastrium, two attacks of bilious vomiting; no stool. General condition good.

Continue *Nux-vomica.*

May 13.—Neither vomiting nor stool. Nose bleed in the morning.

Appetite. Broths.

May 14. Nose-bleed. Convalescence.

Discharged cured May 22d.

CASE XVIII.—*By Dr. Guyton.—Simple Cholera. Died in the cold stage.*

Fugeon, 64 years, admitted May 9th, in the ward Sainte-Anne, No. 22.

She was small, of a bad shape, thin and broken down by age. During yesterday she was attacked with diarrhœa; this morning the vomiting set in, then the cramps, and the coldness.

Admitted at 10 o'clock in the morning. Cholera-features; eyes sunken, dull; lividity around the orbits; blue lips.

Breathing embarrassed, short, hurried; voice very feeble. Pulse collapsed. Cyanosis of the hands, with engorgement of the veins, without circulation on the hands or forearms; cyanosis of the legs. Coldness of the extremities; coldness of the face, neck, upper part of the chest, forearms; all these parts are covered with a clammy sweat.

Tongue violet-colored, without coating, dry; thirst intense. Abdomen drawn in, painful to pressure in the epigastric and umbilical region. Nausea; vomiting after admission, scanty and clear as water. Does in her bed without being conscious of it; the discharges are liquid, do not stain the linen. No urine.

Arsenicum 6, in solution, every hour.

Prostration; frequent and painful cramps in the legs and hands.

Evening.—Same coldness, same cyanosis; no pulse; involuntary stools, no vomiting. Cramps which cause her to moan. The patient is sinking.

May 10.—The patient has been sinking ever since she came to the hospital; there never was a sign of reaction.

In the morning the lividity was more marked; the skin perfectly cold, moist, without elasticity. Involuntary stools.

In the middle of the day, the patient became insensible; grasping at flocks and coma set in, and she died at 7 o'clock in the evening.

CASE XIX.—*By Dr. Guyton.—Simple Cholera. —Cure.*

Kolsch, 44 years old, mason, admitted May 10th, ward St. Benjamin.

Three days ago he was attacked with diarrhœa without

any apparent cause ; frequent liquid discharges, without colic. The first two days the patient was able to work ; yesterday he was taken with weakness, loss of appetite, malaise. In the evening the vomiting set in, cramps at night.

May 10.—Cholera-features ; sunken eyes with lividity around the orbits, lips and chin.

Breathing difficult, hurried ; voice falsified rather than weak. Pulse very small, frequent and disappearing under the least pressure. Coldness of the extremities, and more particularly of the face, neck, upper part of the chest, covered with a cold and clammy moisture. Cyanosis of the extremities ; the veins on the hands and forearms look blue, they are bloated, the circulation is arrested.

Tongue livid, coated white, moist ; intense thirst ; acute pain in the epigastric and umbilical regions with or without pressure ; abdomen drawn in. Frequent turns of liquid vomiting, the last is like water. Several stools. No urine since last night.

Mind perfectly clear. Strength good ; some restlessness, frontal headache ; frequent and painful cramps in the legs and hands.

Veratrine 3, in solution ; water and sugar ; warm flannels.

Evening.—The patient has warmed up ; a pretty strong reaction has set in ; the skin is warm, but not uniformly ; the face remains cool, the tongue cold ; no sweat. Pulse pretty full, frequent. Thirst intense. Constant and intense pains at the epigastrium, aggravated by pressure and by drawing breath ; nausea ; five times the patient vomited up a rose-colored liquid, probably mixed with a little blood. No stool ; no urine.

Breathing hurried, short, labored ; the patient complains of painful constriction at the base of the thorax. Headache, restlessness ; cramps at short intervals.

Arsenicum 6, in solution, every hour, three spoonfuls only; followed by *Carbo-veg*. 6, in solution, every hour.

May 11.—The patient feels easier this morning; the breathing is still frequent, but easier; the voice is sound. The cyanosis of the hands is less; pulse full and frequent. Tongue moist, warm; a good deal of thirst. Acute pain in the epigastrium; nausea; five times he vomited up a brown liquid with a red precipitate, evidently blood. No stool, no urine.

Nux-vomica 3, in solution.

Evening.—Marked improvement. Respiration fuller, less hurried; good temperature of the skin; no cyanosis of the hands; pulse full, not frequent. The eyes are still sunken and surrounded with blue rings, but the countenance has resumed its natual expression. Some headache. Tongue moist, almost natural. Thirst moderate; some nausea, no vomiting; sensitiveness of the epigastrium, not exactly a pain. No stool, no urine; every now and then the patient experiences an urging at the anus. Had two or three naps in the day-time.

May 12.—Good sleep. Features almost natural. No lividity round the eyes, which continue somewhat sunken. Breathing easy, not frequent. Warmth and pulse normal.

Tongue coated white, moist; some thirst. Sensitiveness at the epigastrium; no nausea, vomiting or stool. The urinary secretion is restored. No return of the cramps.

Continue *Nux-vomica.*

May 13.—Scanty bilious stool in the day-time. Appetite. Broths.

May 14.—Thick stool. Decidedly convalescent.

May 18.—Discharged cured.

This case shows a well marked gastritis during the period of reaction; it yielded speedily to Nux-vomica.

CASE XX.—*By Dr. Guyton.—Simple Cholera. —Cure.*

Toupin, 29 years old, a mason, admitted May 10th, ward St. Benjamin, No. 11.

On the 5th of May the patient was taken with diarrhœa; next day continued his work.

May 7.—Was taken with vomiting, cramps, coldness.

May 8.—A physician was sent for; he ordered six leeches at the epigastrium, Seltzers' water and an anti-emetic. The vomiting and diarrhœa continue.

May 10.—The patient is taken to the hospital, and arrived when the physician was making his rounds.

Marked emaciation, sunken eyes, livid complexion and blueish lips.

Breathing anxious, frequent, voice feeble. The pulse is small, hurried; the upper surfaces of the hands and feet look spotted. The temperature is lower than in a state of health, but not sunken to the coldness of cholera; a reaction is evidently approaching. Tongue cold, rather dry, coated white; intense thirst. Abdomen drawn in, the epigastric and umbilical regions are painful with or without pressure.

Repeated vomiting and stools. No urine.

Mind perfect, weakness; restlessness, headache. Frequent cramps.

Veratrine 3, in solution; water and sugar; warm flannels.

Increase of temperature in the evening; the skin feels warm, the pulse is full, rather large, hurried. Tongue cool, rather dry; thirst. Nausea; four turns of vomiting, with a greenish tinge. No stool since his admission; pain at the epigastrium.

Breathing frequent; headache; continued restlessness. The cramps occur but seldom. No urine.

May 11.—General improvement; better temperature, more uniform; pulse less frequent, fuller; no cyanosis. Tongue moist, slightly coated white; thirst moderate The pain at the epigastrium continues; nausea. No vomiting or stool. Two emissions of urine in the night.

Less restlessness; the breathing is easier and the voice has returned. Less headache; nose-bleed in the morning.

Carbo-veg. in solution.

May 12.—Sleeps in the night; no headache. Feels generally comfortable. Breathing, temperature and pulse natural.

No pain at the epigastrium; no vomiting, no stool. Has some difficulty in urinating. Appetite.

Carbo-veg. in solution. Broths.

May 13.—No vomiting or stool. Nose-bleed.

Broths, wine of Bagnolles.

May 14.—Completely convalescent. Discharged cured May 18th.

This was a very simple case of cholera. No dangerous symptoms in the cold stage; no serious symptoms during the reaction; the convalescence was rapid and easy.

We stated in the commencement that the treatment of cholera can be established on a truly scientific basis: we have given twenty cases of this treatment. This is not sufficient to demonstrate the proposition which we have advanced. The method which had been followed, has to be explained. By method we mean the general principle which directed in each case the application of positive remedies to particular diseases. But, inasmuch as every body pretends to practice a rational system of medicine, or to base therapeutics upon positive indications, it behooves us to show in what manner a scientific system of therapeutics differs from one that is arbitrary, or in what manner indications and medications that are positive and based upon experience, differ from such as are purely hypothetical. Both these methods have been applied to the treatment of cholera;

we are enabled to analyse, compare and judge them. It is after having instituted such a comparison that we determined to adopt the one in preference to the other, and to treat our patients accordingly. We shall give our reasons for so doing. Let us first explain the method prescribed by the rational, hypothetic, *classical* medicine. This method involves a variety of modes: Some understand by indications the explanations which they give of the disease; others have adopted certain routine indications for every disease, which correspond to five or six different forms of medication. Others prescribe a different medicine for every single symptom; others again base their therapeutic indications upon the essence or the unknown and inscrutable cause of the disease, and seek for the specific remedy whose unknown action is to triumph over the unknown nature of the malady. All these various forms of treatment have been resorted to in the management of cholera.

According to Broussais cholera is gastro-enteritis; every inflammation has to be combated by sanguineous emissions; hence cholera, being an inflammatory disease, has to be treated by every kind of antiphlogistics. According to others, cholera consists in a relaxed condition of the pores of the bowels; this view leads us, therefore, to the use of astringents. The only trouble is to find a suitable astringent that is willing to accomplish this use.

Some look upon cholera as a case of poisoning. If this were true, the treatment would depend upon the nature of the poison; but this is not so. According to the adherents of this hypothesis, cholera results from the action of some unknown poison upon the animal economy. It is therefore unnecessary to trouble one's-self about the antidote; only, since the poison has necessarily entered the circulation, we have to drive it out thence by every possible channel, and, to this effect, excite all the secretions. In this respect it is supposed that we simply imitate nature: do we not see nature open the pores of the stomach and of the bowels, drive out the poisonous matter by the mouth and the anus, &c.? This system is the opposite of the preceding one, which aims at closing the relaxed pores and arresting the excessive use which nature is making of her curative resources.

The modern hippocratist is no more embarrassed by the cholera than by any other disease. According to him there are no diseases, there are only patients.

If the patient exhibits signs of plethora, he is bled. If he has too much bile, he is vomited and purged. If his strength fails him, give him tonics. If an ataxic condition sets in, he is treated with nervines. If there is a certain intermission in the symptoms, do not fail to give him quinine.

This method is so much the more positive that it applies to every form of disease, or rather to all sorts of patients. He who has acquired the art of *manœuvring* (this is the consecrated term) with these few remedies is a practitioner of consummate skill, a man of positive and sure mind, of sound judgment ..... The pharmaceutic appliances may be varied a good deal. There is a more or less well filled arsenal of antiphlogistics, emetics, purgatives, tonics, nervines, antiperiodic medicines, &c. Art, which is an imitation of nature, ought to be as accommodating and varied in its proceedings as nature herself is disposed to modify the infinite variety of her phenomena. It is by this sort of scientific jargon that they color the ordinary routine practice, based upon half a dozen indications drawn from a hard pulse, a coated tongue, &c. The symptom-practice is that which is most generally in vogue. It consists in treating each symptom separately by some particular remedy. This leads to a therapeutic confusion, a sort of chaos in the midst of which the physician becomes entangled in a network of uncertainties, and the poor patient is pulled about in every direction. If he gets well, it is impossible to tell what cured him; if he dies, it is equally impossible to determine what destroyed him. In the management the symptom-practice is applied as follows:

In the first period:

For the coldness: warm cloths, warm air-baths.

For the thirst: ice, cold water, or stimulating hot drinks.

For the vomiting: Seltzer's water, anti-vomiting medicines.

For the diarrhœa: opiate-injections, astringents.

For the cramps: dry frictions, or frictions with various liniments.

For the collapse of pulse: stimulating drinks, aromatics, cordials, tonics.

In the second period:

For the fever and the congestions: general bleeding, cupping, leeches.

If the congestions continue: revulsives, vesicatories, diuretics.

If some symptom of the former period should remain: the same treatment that had been resorted to at first.

Moreover every physician has some favorite remedies which he likes to make use of in every case.

As regards the specific treatment of cholera, its partizans, who are as yet searching for the true specific of this disease, employ alternately every thing which credulity or the thirst for lucre had brought into vogue as a remedy for the most desperate cases of cholera, and which had proved to be as infallible as any remedy for a common cold. As soon as the cholera breaks out any where, it is at once preceded by the announcement of specifics. While the epidemic prevails, the specific remedies succeed each other. Every day some new specific takes the place of one that had been abondoned. Towards the close of the disease, the specifics are forgotten. This does not eradicate the mania for specifics; for those who are affected with it, go in search of other specifics.

This criticism of methods which are founded upon arbitrary indications, seems severe; it is only just, however, as every one will admit who has a proper knowledge of the insufficiency of the remedial means with which the cholera has been treated: indeed, the most intelligent and the most experienced practitioners are of my opinion. I am, no more than they, willing to impeach without limitation the use of empirical or symptomatic indications. With a little tact the errors of these methods are not only avoided, but may be used to some good purpose. Instead of acting upon all the symptoms simultaneously, the principal ones only might be taken as leading indications; by this means contradictory medications would be avoided; nevertheless, this kind of treatment would lack a positive basis, and the mind would remain wavering and dissatisfied.

But to say, as Broussois does, that cholera is a gastro-enteritis, is simply to take advantage of a few cases where the symptoms of gastro-enteritis are evident, in order to declare that inflammation is the constant and leading character of the disease. Supposing even that this inflammation is as regular a symptom in cholera as it is in typhus, this does not show that the former can be rightfully considered as a true form of inflammation, for this reason: that cholera lacks the common characteristics of an inflammatory disease, such as result from the relation of the fever to the local alteration, from the condition of the blood, the course of the phenomena, &c. And even, if cholera really were a genuine form of inflammation, this would not necessarily justify an antiphlogistic treatment. The treatment adopted in one form of inflammation, does not determine the treatment to be adopted in another form. The treatment of pneumonia is no criterium for that of bronchitis, nor does the treatment of bronchitis establish a precedent for that of ophthalmia. Phlegmonous inflammation may have to be treated differently from erysipelas. One of the serious errors of our art consists in establishing a general method of treatment for a whole class of diseases, antiphlogistics for inflammations, astringents for blennorrhœa, antispasmodics for spasms. This is the most deplorable abuse that could be made of the principle of analogy; and it is still more absurd to designate by the name of inflammation any disease that presents inflammatory symptoms, and to allow such a fanciful definition to lead one to the use of antiphlogistics in the management of this malady. Broussais' method is therefore false in theory; in 1832 we have seen what it was worth in the treatment of cholera. To say that the cholera disease proceeds from a relaxation of the bowels or the glands of the stomach, is to use a mere word in the place of a scientific solution. In pathological anatomy, the term *relaxation* is synonymous with *prolapsus*. To say in physiology or pathology that the increase of a secretion depends upon a relaxation, and then, under cover of this doctrine, to prescribe *astringents*, in other words, drugs, the effects of which are not known, is simply to cover a fallacy by an absurdity, instead of treating, a disease by a remedy. Is it rational medicine to inflict upon patients the consequences of a double sophism?

I have been sufficiently explicit in speaking of the hippocratic treatment of cholera, such as it was proposed and conducted by Double in 1832, to dispense with all further criticism on this head. It matters little with what apparent depth the theory of the morbid elements of cholera may be expounded as a basis for therapeutic indications and methods: these elements are none the the less fanciful creations which are just as dangerous in a therapeutic as they are absurd in a pathological point of view. This theory leads to a nosography which is just as superficial as its corresponding method of treatment. This is evident from the following passage of the *General Pathology* of Professor Chomel: "If it is impossible, as it would seem to be according to the useless efforts of nosographists, to obtain a uniform rule for the classification of all diseases* such a classification should undoubtedly be based upon the highest possible considerations of usefulness, and the varieties of every disease should be arranged with a view to securing the best possible treatment. In all acute disease it is, in our opinion, the inflammatory, bilious, mucous, adynamic or ataxic character which should determine the treatment; for the character is just as important to the treatment as the class to which the disease belongs. Should a disease, no matter to what class it belongs, present the general symptoms of an inflammatory fever, bleeding and antiphlogistic regime have to be resorted to; adynamic diseases should be treated with stimulants and tonics; simple diseases, which have neither an inflammatory nor adynamic character, and are not otherwise complicated with heterogeneous phenomena, may not require any medicine; rest and a light diet are sometimes sufficient to remove them; and even these means are not always necessary, as we see in measles, erysipelas, pulmonary catarrh, &c."

The result of this theory of the forms, indications and modes of treatment of acute diseases, is an extreme

* Why insist upon a uniform rule to distinguish the forms of each disease? Who says, that all diseases must have the same forms? Chemists even do not search for a uniform re-agens in all cases, nor a uniform mode of combination. Why should physicians, instead of determining the form of every disease by observation, undertake to determine these forms by guess-work?

simplification of the healing art. *The greatest use* would seem to consist in not studying acute diseases. It is sufficient to be able to distinguish the inflammatory, bilious, mucous, adynamic and ataxic character, in order to decide whether the disease with which the patient is affected, has one of these characters, and to regulate the treatment accordingly. Indeed, if none of these characters exists, *rest and a light diet are most generally all that is required for a cure** of what use are nosology and diagnosis?

This is what they term classic medicine. This kind of medicine was applied to the treatment of cholera as rational medicine! inflammatory, bilious, mucous, adynamic and ataxic character, &c.! Is it too much to say that the mind of the physician does not find any thing in these common indications and methods that could serve him as guide? I think not.

I shall say nothing either of the symptomatic or the specific method of treatment.

If I am not mistaken, neither the rational system of therapeutics nor the rational treatment of cholera sustain a serious examination. If experience had confirmed in any way these hypothetical and arbitrary methods of treatment, experience might be appealed to as a witness; but it seems to me that the last epidemic has left the minds still more sceptical than the epidemic of 1832.

Is Hahnemann's method more scientific? I believe this can be shown.

It is well known that, according to Hahnemann, the totality of the symptoms determines the remedy to be employed; and that this remedy must be capable of producing in the healthy body a morbid condition that

* And if all these conditions should be insufficient, (which is generally the case) it is doubtless unnecessary to trouble one's-self about the disease at all. How easy it is to simplify the healing art with a little more or a little less!

is exactly similar to the natural disease. This correspondence between the remedy and the disease constitutes the spirit and the foundation of the Hahnemannean system. Hence the resemblance between the drug-disease and the natural malady cannot be too minute. There might not be any thing arbitrary either in the observation of the symptoms or in the determination of the remedy.

In order to establish scientifically the condition of the patient, we have to know in the first place the nature of his disease, and then proceed to individualize the case before us. If we only consider the disease, the indication would be too general to enable us to adapt the remedy to this particular case. If, on the other hand, we lose sight of the disease, and only record the symptoms without reference to their physiological connection, we only obtain a confused image of the malady, and can at most only proceed empirically in the treatment. Indeed, all we can know of the previous condition of the patient, in that which is related to us by himself and those with him; and the future developments of the disease remain hidden from our reason. In this state of affairs the physician is reduced to the necessity of improvising a certain group of phenomena, and cônnecting them together empirically; for he has no means of classifying them according to their relative importance and pathological bearing. Even if a perfect resemblance between the phenomena of the disease and the symptoms of the remedy existed, this would not be conclusive; for, shortly after, some of the symptoms might become worse or disappear altogether, so that the physician, in order to do justice to his patient, would have to remain by his bedside all the time, watch every little change that might occur, and modify the treatment accordingly.

If behooves us to follow the good sense of all ages, and, recognising the truth of an essential principle of disease, regard both the disease and the patient; neither believe with the hippocratists that there are only patients, nor with the partizans of the specific method, that there are only diseases.*

From our standing-point the morbid indications are based upon all the light that nosography, etiology, semeiotics and pathological anatomy are capable of shedding upon the character of the disease. Each of the morbid phenomena, studied in itself and in its relations with the other phenomena, occupies its appropriate place in the whole series of symptoms. The present series is naturally connected with the past and the prospective character of the disease. The disease appears to us as an evolution of phenomena that was known and foreseen. We are not exposed to the danger of mistaking for drug-symptoms changes that are natural developments of the disease. In one word, we treat disease scientifically instead of applying a mathematical formula like a blind man.

In cholera we have distinguished four varieties. Each variety has moreover various degrees, phases, periods; each period is characterized by a peculiar group of symptoms; finally the cholera-disease may assume a peculiar epidemic type, and this type may manifest itself by distinctive phenomena.

As regards the patient, each patient exhibits peculiar conditions of sex, age, constitution, habits, regime, idio-

* Hahnemann rejects as chimerical every indication which is drawn from the essential nature of the disease; in my estimation, this is an absolute error, and, in every respect, fraught with mischief. In proclaiming with certain adherents of the hippocratic method the doctrine, that there are only patients, and that disease is not an essential state of the organism, the author of homœopathy has rejected the only truth which can secure a scientific basis to pathology. Inasmuch as not any one truth can be opposed to any other, it is our belief that the doctrine to which we vow allegiance, can be reconciled with Hahnemann's method, and that his reform can be grafted upon a truly scientific system of pathology.

syncrasy; and he may have contracted the disease under the influence of some particular cause.

The two categories include every possible source from which we can draw our indications.

1. Indication drawn from the disease itself.

After having studied the cholera-disease in its various forms and having discovered the leading character of the disturbance, or the phenomenon which, on account of its importance and constant recurrence, seems to constitute the very centre of the disease, we arrive at this conclusion, that cholera is, in its fundamental nature, an affection of the stomach and bowels, as its name indicates. It is therefore of the utmost importance correctly to determine the *nature* of this affection, provided we understand by nature no more than is intended, namely: the pathological character of the disease.

This affection of the digestive canal, in cholera, extends throughout the whole extent of its mucous lining, from the mouth to the large intestine inclusively. The pathognomonic signs of this affection vary, however, according to the various regions of the body where they are examined.

In the mouth it is a catarrhal irritation, generally affecting the whole cavity, and characterized by a swelling and redness of the upper border of the gums, the mucous membrane of the lips, of the edges and lower surface of the tongue, and by a thick mucous coating on the upper surface of this organ. In some cases we perceive a real inflammation of the buccal cavity from the very commencement of the disease; it is known by an inflammatory streak along the gums, by a pseudo-membranous layer extending over the convex surface of the gums, by irregular patches on the dorsum of the tongue, and by an acute redness and swelling of its edges. During the cold period the buccal cavity is moist; but as soon as the reaction has set in, the dryness, the cracking, the rhagades and the swelling of these parts leave no doubt as to the inflammatory character of the affection. In some rare cases the inflammation is intense, accompanied by diphtheritic patches, which extend even to the mucous lining of the cheeks. In one case I have seen this inflammation extend from the parietal mucous lining to the parotid, with inflammation of this gland, as we see it in the stomatitis of typhus, and in certain forms of stomatitis, of old people. This mechanism of the development of parotitis is, in our judgment, one of the many proofs of the truth of the theory which we have presented in our inaugural dissertation. (Theses of 1836), that an inflammation develops itself by vascular layers.

The fauces likewise exhibit an acute redness, which is sometimes accompanied by thin and loosely adhering membranous patches, sometimes extending low down in the œsophogus. Is the aphonia of cholera-patients to be attributed to this congested or inflammatory condition of the lining membrane down to the vocal chords? I do not pretend to say; I have thought of this too late to verify this idea by post-mortem examinations.

I have purposely dwelt upon this buccal inflammation because it is almost universally overlooked. The tongue is still examined as it was at a period when its coating was accounted for by the convenient theory of the humors, and this loose examination is considered satisfactory, instead of exploring the buccal cavity in its whole extent, which would probably furnish a clue to the condition of the tongue.

The stomach, especially toward the cordia, is the seat of an acute catarrhal irritation; I ought to add that sanguineous infiltrations and a dotted appearance are discovered in this organ, which only belong to a state of inflammation. The pain in the epigastrium, the internal heat, the vomiting which is at first bilious, then serous, then bilious and bitter during the reaction; the excessive sensitiveness of the stomach to the action of natural excitants, such as a little broth at the commencement of the remission which precedes convalescence: all these symptoms together go to show that the gastric affection is something more than a hyper-secretion, and that there is either a state of catarrhal or inflammatory irritation of the gastric mucous membrane. I am well aware that, if we mean to accommodate ourselves to the prejudices of *observers*, we must not talk any longer of inflammation of the stomach in acute diseases. But these observers having forgotten to define the signs by which the presence or absence of an inflammation of the mucous membrane can be known, we look upon their assertions as purely fictitious, as pathological anatomy of the sentimental order.*

The intestinal affection, which is very distinct in the duodenum, generally diminishes in the jejunum, where it ceases to be continuous, and is scattered over large surfaces. In the ileum, the inflammation manifests itself by the development of the mucous follicles, and the prominence of Peyer's glands, with or without swelling of the corresponding mesenteric ganglions. In this portion of the intestines the dotted appearance still continues, together with softened points and little superficial ulcerations. The cœcum generally presents an appearance of catarrhal irritation, seldom of inflammation. As a general rule, the colon is not much affected; nevertheless, the lower part of this bowel is sometimes the seat of superficial inflammation which manifests itself during life by mucous stools of a dysenteric character.

I have no remarks to offer concerning the nature of the alvine discharges. I may however point out the progressive suppression of the bile in these evacuations, and its reappearance after the cold stage is over.

* An observer in pathological anatomy should not content himself with simply saying no, where Broussais has said *yes*.

These are the characteristic signs of the cholera affection in the digestive passages: 1. general catarrhal irritation: 2. catarrhal irritations and partial inflammations scattered all over the mucous lining of the alimentary canal.

This affection belongs to all the forms of the disease. It is seen in every stage. This led Broussais to look upon cholera as an inflammation of the stomach and bowels. But there are cases where the inflammation is wanting, and where even the catarrhal irritation is not always proportionate to the intensity of the other symptoms. This shows that cholera cannot always be considered as an inflammatory disease without committing a double error.

The first element in the indications of the disease is, as we have shown, the affection of the digestive organs.

Another element consists in the ulceration of the phenomena of exhalation, secretion and nutrition. After the physiological analysis which we have offered, it seems unnecessary to dwell any further upon this point.

The third element of our indications is suggested by the condition of the vital functions.

And the fourth, by the pains, cramps, restlessness, and other subjective symptoms.

2. Indications drawn from the forms of the disease.

By classifying the phenomena of the various forms of cholera, each agreeably to its own character, these forms may lead us to establish with more correctness and precision the therapeutic character of the disease, and the appropriate means of cure.

In diarrhœic cholera, commonly termed cholerine, the gastro-intestinal affection constitutes pretty much the whole disease; the therapeutic indications are principally based upon the condition of the alimentary canal. The disorders in the reproductive system, or any other symptom that may exist conjointly with the digestive disturbance, should, however, likewise be noticed.

In simple cholera, the order of the symptoms is a thing of importance; by means of it we are enabled to trace the successive invasion of the organs performing the functions of digestion, nutrition, circulation, hæmatosis, animation and co-ordination.

In ataxic cholera, we have to add to the totality of the symptoms a new element, namely: the absence of all regularity in the combination or succession of the morbid phenomena.

In black cholera, the simultaneous appearance and the intensity of the symptoms constitutes a chief indication.

3. Every form has its periods which the physician should not lose sight of, since the totality of the phenomena varies in the different stages of disease. The phenomena of the period of reaction differ from those of the cold period. The febrile motion gradually takes the place of coldness and vital depression: nevertheless, in this stage, the gastro-intestinal affection continues to act a prominent part; sometimes it is even the source of new indications. Lastly, isolated phenomena may develop themselves after the remission, and invite the attention of the physician. This remark likewise applies to the secondary phenomena in the convalescent stage.

These last-mentioned phenomena are on a par with the precursory symptoms, the importance of which has been pointed out with so much clearness by Dr. Guérin. In this case the indications are almost entirely confined to the digestive canal; nevertheless it must not be forgotten that the precursory symptoms sometimes consist in some simple nervous derangement, which, however, should be treated with the same care as the alvine discharges.

4. It is useful to note the causa occasionalis of an attack of cholera; nevertheless, the importance of such causes is much less in epidemic than in sporadic cholera.

5. The sex, age, constitution, idiosyncracies, regimen and habits of the patient, may furnish us special indications.

Having agreed upon the indications, we have now to determine the corresponding treatment. This treatment consists, according to Hahnemann in administering such drugs as are capable of producing in the healthy organism a disturbance similar to the natural cholera-disease. Supposing this law to be true, it is evident that it can only be applied on condition that we should possess a series of drug-symptoms exactly analogous to the symptoms of the natural malady. In the present condition of the homœopathic materia-medica there are still considerable deficiencies, and not all therapeutic indications can be satisfied. Hahnemann's method, if applied to the treatment of cholera, seems as yet limited and circumscribed in its sphere of action. This method is brilliantly successful in cholerine and in simple cholera. In ataxic and black cholera it seems comparatively powerless, because we have no drug in our materia-medica the effects of which upon the healthy organism correspond to the totality of the symptoms in either of these forms. Inasmuch as either of them generally terminates fatally, it is easy to determine beforehand the good or bad result of the homœopathic treatment in a case of cholera. The cures under this treatmeat are generally cases of diarrhœic and normal cholera, excepting however a few cases of old persons who sink in the period of convalescence, and such patients as are brought to the hospital in a state of collapse. The number of deaths generally corresponds to the number of cases of black and ataxic cholera. During the epidemic of 1849 I have only seen one case of either of these forms get well. All the other cases failed as I had seen them fail in 1832; only the relative number of cases was different; in 1832 the black cholera prevailed at the commencement of the epidemic; in 1849 ataxic cholera was more frequent than the black form. This difference was sufficient to impart a distinctive character to the two epidemics. The irregularity in the course of the reaction, which is always incomplete in the ataxic form, has surprized the physicians who expect to see a consistent febrile reaction set in after the cold period is terminated.

These relative differences are of very little consequence so far as the treatment is concerned, inasmuch as these two categories of patients succomb almost always under any kind of treatment.*

In those forms of cholera where medical treatment seems to have at all any effect, the Hahnemannean method is preferable to the ordinary methods; and is both more scientific and more efficacious. May we hope that therapeutic agents will yet be discovered that shall produce a simile of the cholera-disease in the healthy organism? This hope is legitimate, and we ought to search for such agents.

The twenty cases which I have related, show what medicines correspond to cholera and normal cholera. The same medicines proved powerless in the other varieties, except in one case of ataxic cholera, where the vital forces, instead of sinking, were roused.

The attenuations which we have used, were generally

* It seems fair to treat the black and ataxic forms of cholera in the usual manner, inasmuch as homœopathy fails completely in either of these varieties. I had seen in 1832 that the ordinary methods were just as powerless. In 1849 I again employed the same treatment after having convinced, myself that the homœopathic treatment was inefficient *except in a very few cases*. But the most powerful allœopathic treatment did not produce any better results. This reveals to us an absolute want which is unfortunately common to all methods.

lower than those used in pneumonia.* The medicines taken from the mineral kingdom, were used at the 6th attenuation; those taken from the vegetable kingdom, at the third. Of Camphor the alcoholic spirits were used. When a medicine was given in solution, a drop of the third or sixth attenuation was mixed in from 4 to 6 oz. of filtered water (about half a pint,) of such mixtures a tablespoonful was given every five, ten, fifteen or twenty minutes, according as the symptoms seemed to be more or less urgent. In proportion as the patient improved the intervals between the doses were prolonged to one or two hours.

Here follows a list of the remedies which correspond to the indications that we have furnished.

In the precursory stage, when it is as yet impossible to determine the true form of the disease, we have not only to note the sensations and pains experienced by the patient, but also the causes which may have more directly occasioned the outbreak of the disease, such as: excesses, moral emotions, &c.

According to the nature of the symptoms and the circumstances in which the cholera had broken out, the following medicines will be found effectual:

Chamomilla-vulgaris;
Nux-vomica;
Pulsatilla;
Carbo-vegetabilis;
Ipecacuanha;
Phosphorus;
Secale-cornutum;
Phosphori-acidum.

Cholerine often gets well of itself, but it is better to treat it medicinally. Besides it is sometimes very difficult to distinguish an attack of cholerine from the precursory stage of one of the serious forms of cholera.

* See Clinical Remarks on Pneumonia, by the same Author. New-York, Wm. Radde.

Agreeably to the indications, the first period requires:

Ipecacuanha;
Phosphori-acidum;
Veratrum.

The second period:

Aconitum-napellus;
Nux-vomica;
Pulsatilla;
China;
Sulphur;
Camphora.

Normal or simple cholera requires in the first period:

Ipecacuanha;
Phosphorus;
Phosphori-acidum.

In the period of growth or increase:

Nux-vomica;
Veratrum;
Arsenicum.

If Ipecac. or Nux-vomica are not sufficient to arrest the disease, we must not lose any time in giving Veratrum; and if the phenomena still continue, resort to Arsenicum. At the close of the epidemic I gave the Arsenic at once in simple cholera, and this treatment seemed to me preferable to blind experimentation with Nux-vomica, Ipecacuanha or even Veratrum. This last named remedy was often found sufficient in mild cases. Arsenic triumphed in the severer cases of genuine cholera. So that these three drugs: Ipecacuanha, Veratrum and Arsenicum answer to three different degrees of true cholera. At the commencement of the epidemic I was in the habit of alternating either of these remedies with Carbo-vegetabilis, to meet the depression of vital and natural strength. Afterwards I gave up this alternating method, because it hides the genuine effects of each drug, and I only gave vegetable charcoal when it was indicated by the symptoms either in the first or second period.

The period of reaction frequently proved to be a perfect remission of the disease, which often led to convalescence. If this was not the case, I gave, in accordance with the perceptible phenomena:

Aconitum-napellus;
Ipecacuanha;
Camphora;
Carbo-vegetabilis;
Belladonna;
Mercurius;
Nux-vomica;
Pulsatilla;
Cina.

Secondary phenomena sometimes yielded to China, at other times to Sulphur, to Calcarea or to Nux-vomica.

To understand the use of these drugs in cholera, their effects upon a person in health have first to be known. These effects may be studied in Hahnemann's Materia Medica, and in Jahr's Symptomen-Codex.*

I will now mention the principal remedies which I have found most frequently indicated.

As regards the black or ataxic cholera, I am sorry to say that I cannot propose any effectual mode of treatment. We have no drug that presents in their totality the phenomena of black cholera, no remedy that presents at the same time the symptoms of cholera, and a condition of ataxy or malignity, that is to say, an incoherence of the morbid symptoms, a depression of the vital and natural forces, and a deep derangement of the animal functions.

Wherever medical treatment is possible, Hahnemann's method admits of a scientific determination of the thera-

* Translated by Charles J. Hempel, M.D., and published by W. Radde, 322 Broadway, New-York.

peutic indications and the treatment of cholera. But this method does not fill up the chasm formed by the ataxic and black varieties.

This, at any rate, is my experience derived from the treatment of about a hundred cases during the epidemic of 1849. Hahnemann's method has seemed to me more efficacious than any of the other methods of treatment. So far as this can be shown by figures, figures do show this. Under the Hahnemannean method about one-tenth recovered more than under any other. Under the ordinary methods from 59 to 60 out of every 100 died in each of the wards of the hospital Sainte-Marguérite, where cholera patients were received; and under the Hahnemannean method only from 48 to 49 out of every hundred. I mention these figures for the purpose of refuting certain hazardous conclusions drawn from the trial made of Hahnemann's method by my colleague and friend, Doctor Natalis Guillot, physician to the Salpêtrière, in seven of the most desperate cases of his ward, where indeed every case was desperate. He was prevented from continuing his experiments, in consequence of a little vial labelled Arsenicum having been seen, which gave rise to the report that he poisoned his patients and which produced a terrible commotion among the people. It would have been more honorable and more scientific to study the effects of Hahnemann's method on the cholera-patients of my wards in Sainte-Marguérite than to distort the incipient experiments at the Salpêtrière which had to be given up by force. Even if Hahnemann's method were absolutely false, its falsity ought to be shown by candid and logical arguments.

Hahnemann's method enables us to establish the therapeutic indications and modes of treatment in cholera upon a scientific basis. In the present condition of the homœopathic Materia Medica, we are as yet unable to combat either the ataxic or the black variety of cholera by adequate remedical agents.*

GENERAL CONCLUSION.

Between the physicians of different creeds and schools, there can only exist one bond in common, that of observation. And this bond really does exist, for we all consider observation or experience as the sole legitimate criterium in medical science. A public and authentic application of this criterium has been so far denied to the homœopathic method. I have not wished to be implicated in such an act of injustice which would be an everlasting dishonor to the medical body, if only a single spark of truth were contained in Hahnemann's doctrine.

I have presented facts before my readers which are well capable of freeing their minds from great prejudices and removing thick scales from their eyes. I have as much as possible acted the part of a historian, and have contented myself with appealing to the intelligence of my readers by facts. Will this lead physicians out of the narrow and selfish ways of their professional business to the nobler and generous platform of scientific observation? This is to be hoped.

The treatment of pneumonia and cholera is a severe trial for a new system of therapeutics. I have said perhaps too little regarding the former malady; I feel as though I had done injustice to homœopathy by an exaggerated feeling of reserve. Every day I establish by new facts, the efficacy of phosphorus and Bryonia in this severe disease, where, according to the statistics of Dr. Louis, 32 die out of every 106 pa-

* It is possible that the nitrate of silver, concerning which Dr. Barth has made some interesting investigations, may fill up a portion of this gap in the treatment of cholera. The results of his inquiries were not known to us until after the epidemic, so that it was impossible to put them to the test of experience.

tients. I prefer however remaining within the bounds of truth, than to go beyond them. I have avoided to pronounce an absolute judgment on the merits of Hahnemann's system; my aim has been to convince my colleagues of the necessity of not condemning this therapeutic method in virtue of a pretended patent-right in science, instead of studying it by careful observation. Man is not endowed with intuition; in the natural sciences nothing is known with exactness except by observation. "Man," says Pascal, "is neither an angel nor a brute; and it unfortunately happens, that the man who wants to act like an angel, generally behaves like an irrational brute." It is well to profit by this advice.

CATALOGUE

OF

HOMŒOPATHIC BOOKS

FOR SALE BY

WILLIAM RADDE, 322 BROADWAY, NEW-YORK,

PUBLISHER OF HOMŒOPATHIC BOOKS AND SOLE AGENT FOR THE LEIPZIG CENTRAL HOMŒOPATHIC PHARMACY.

Guernsey's Homœopathic Domestic Practice. With full descriptions of the dose to each single case. Containing also Chapters on Anatomy, Physiology, Hygiene, and an Abridged Materia Medica 1854. Third thousand. Bound, $1 50.

☞ Dr. Guernsey's book of Domestic Practice is a reliable and useful work. It is especially adapted to the service of well educated heads of families.—JOHN F. GRAY, M. D.

Bryant, Dr. J., A Pocket Manual or Repertory of Homœopathic Medicine, alphabetically and nosologically arranged; which may be used as the physician's Vade-Mecum, the traveller's Medical Companion, or the Family Physician: containing the principal remedies for the most important diseases, symptoms, sensations, characteristics of diseases, &c.; with the principal pathogenetic effects of the medicines on the most important organs and functions of the body; together with diagnosis, explanation of technical terms, directions for the selection and exhibition of remedies, rules of diet, &c., &c. Compiled from the best homœopathic authorities. Bound, $1. 25.

Caspari's Homœopathic Domestic Physician, edited by F. Hartmann, M. D., "Author of the Acute and Chronic Diseases." Translated from the eighth German edition, and enriched by a Treatise on Anatomy and Physiology, embellished with 30 illustrations by W. P. Esrey, M. D. With additions and a preface by C. Hering, M. D. Containing also a Chapter on Mesmerism and Magnetism; directions for patients living some distance from a homœopothic physician, to describe their symptoms; a Tabular Index of the medicines and the diseases in which they are used; and a Sketch of the Biography of Dr. Samuel Hahnemann, the Founder of Homœopathy. Bound, $1. 25.

Curtis, J. T., M. D., and **J. Lillie, M. D.,** Epitome of Homœopathic Practice. Compiled chiefly from Jahr, Rückert, Beauvais, Bœnninghausen, &c. Second enlarged edition. 1850. Bound, 75 cts.

Douglas, Dr. J. S., Homœopathic Treatment of Intermittent Fevers. 1853. 38 cts.

Dudgeon's Lectures on the Theory and Practice of Homœopathy. Delivered at the Hahnemann Hospital School of Homœopathy, by R. E. Dudgeon, M. D. Manchester, 1854. Bound, (565 pages). $2. 50.

Dysentery and its Homœopathic treatment. Containing also a Repertory and numerous Cases, by F. Humphreys, M. D., Professor of Homœopathic Institutes, Pathology and the Practice of Medicine in the Homœopathic Medical College of Pennsylvania. 1853. Bound, 50 cts.

Esrey, Dr. W. P., Treatise on Anatomy and Physiology. With 30 illustrations. 195 pages. 1851. Bound, 50 cts.

☞ Dr. W. P. Esrey's Treatise on Anatomy and Physiology, is the cheapest book ever published on those subjects, and is particularly of great use to Students of Medicine as a compendium.

Flora Homœopathica; or Illustrations and Descriptions of the Medical Plants used as Homœopathic Remedies. By Edward Hamilton, M. D., F. L. S. The work is illustrated by Henry Sowerby, from Drawings made expressly for the Author. The Flora Homœopathica contains a colored illustration and complete history of every plant generally employed in Homœopathic Pharmacy, arranged in alphabetical order. The drawings are chiefly made from natural specimens, and to ensure correctness, the Author has secured the services of Mr. Henry Sowerby, the Assistant Curator of the Linnean Society. With a Preface, Glossary of Botanical terms and Index. London, 1852. Price for the whole work, containing sixty-six handsomely colored plates, elegantly bound, $18.

Hahnemann, Dr. Samuel, The Lesser Writings of, collected and translated by R. E. Dudgeon, M. D. With a Preface and Notes by E. E. Marcy, M D. With a beautiful steel engraving of Hahnemann, from the statue by Steinhæuser. Bound, one large volume (784 pages), $3. 00.

☞ This valuable work contains a large number of Essays of great interest to laymen as well as medical men, upon diet, the prevention of diseases, ventilation of dwellings, &c. As many of these papers were written before the discovery of the Homœopathic theory of cure, the reader will be enabled to peruse in this volume the ideas of a gigantic intellect when directed to subjects of general and practical interest.

"The Lesser Writings MUST BE READ by every student of Homœopathy who wishes "to become acquainted with the *Master*-mind." R. E. DUDGEON, M. D.

Hempel, Dr. Charles Julius, Complete Repertory of the Homœopathic Materia Medica. Being the third volume of Jahr's New Manual, or Symptomen-Codex, and the most important and complete work ever published, and indispensable for every Homœopathic Practitioner. 1224 pages. 1853. Bound, $6. 00. (See *Jahr's New Manual* or Symptomen-Codex.)

Hempel's *Organon of Specific Homœopathy*, or, an Inductive Exposition of the Principles of the Homœopathic Healing Art, addressed to Physicians and intelligent Laymen, by Charles J. Hempel, M. D, Fellow and Corresponding member of the Homœopathic Medical College of Pennsylvania; Honorary Member of the Hahnemann Society of London, &c. 1854. Bound, $1. 00.

☞ The lecture delivered by the author on the 10th of November of last year, in the Homœopathic Medical College, and which was favorably received, forms a part of the above work.

Jahr, Dr. G. H. G., Diseases of the Skin; or Alphabetical Repertory of the Skin-symptoms and external alterations of substance, together with the morbid phenomena observed in the glandular, osseous, mucous, and circulatory systems, arranged with pathological remarks on the diseases of the skin. Edited by C. J. Hempel, M. D. 1850. Bound, $1.

Jahr's, Dr. G. H. G., and **Possart's** New Manual of the Homœopathic Materia Medica, arranged with reference to well authenticated observations at the sick bed, and accompanied by an alphabetical Repertory, to facilitate and secure the selection of a suitable remedy in any given case. 4th edition, enlarged by the author. SYMPTOMATOLOGY and REPERTORY. Translated and edited by C. J. Hempel, M. D. 1853. Bound, $3. 50.

Laurie's Homœopathic Domestic Medicine. Arranged as a practical work for Students. Containing the treatment of Diseases and a Glossary of medical terms. Sixth American edition, enlarged and improved, by A. Gerald Hull, M. D. 1853. With full descriptions of the dose to each single case. (800 pages) Fourteenth thousand. Bound, $1. 50.

Small, Dr. A. E., Manual of Homœopathic Practice for the use of families and private individuals. 3d edition. 1855. Bound, $2 00.

Small, Dr. A. E., The Pocket Manual of Homœopathic Practice, abridged from the Manual of Homœopathic Practice, by J. F. Sheek, M. D. Bound, 38 cts.

www.ingramcontent.com/pod-product-compliance
Lightning Source LLC
LaVergne TN
LVHW021423110826
845150LV00007B/2053

* 9 7 8 1 4 2 5 5 0 8 5 3 1 *